T^{HE} ★ PRESIDENTS ^{IN} ★
AMERICAN
HISTORY
★ ★ ★

A compact, lively account of each of our
Presidents and his administration, from
George Washington to George H. W.
Bush, followed by a useful Biographical
Digest. The latter presents certain basic
facts about each President, such as the date
and place of his birth, lists all of the Vice
Presidents and cabinet members, and gives
the results of each presidential election.

CHARLES A. BEARD's

THE ★ PRESIDENTS IN ★ AMERICAN HISTORY

★ ★ ★

GEORGE WASHINGTON TO GEORGE BUSH

UPDATED BY **WILLIAM BEARD** AND **DETLEV VAGTS**

JULIAN Ⓜ MESSNER

Library of Congress Cataloging-in-Publication Data

Beard, Charles Austin, 1874-1948.
    Charles A. Beard's the presidents in American
history.

    Summary: Briefly summarizes the achievements of
each presidential administration from Washington to
Bush. Includes a biographical digest giving basic facts
about each president, a list of vice presidents and
cabinet members, and the results of each presidential
election.
    1. Presidents—United States—Biography—Juvenile
literature. 2. United States—Politics and government—
Juvenile literature. [1. Presidents. 2. United States—
Politics and government] I. Beard, William, 1907-
II. Vagts, Detley F. III. Title. IV. Title: Presidents in
American history.
E176.8.B43 1989   973'.09'92   [B]   89-3241
ISBN 0-671-68574-0 (lib.ed.)
ISBN 0-671-68575-9 (pbk.)

PREFACE

★★

This book represents the combined thinking of three generations of an American family who often discussed public affairs together and whose lives, in the aggregate, have spanned more than a century of the country's history. First, my grandfather, Dr. Charles A. Beard (1874–1948), wrote the original edition of *The Presidents in American History* in 1935, and last revised it during Truman's administration. Following his death, his son, William Beard, and daughter, Miriam Vagts, wrote periodic revisions, the last of which was published in 1981, early in Reagan's first term. As Charles Beard's grandson, I now again have the pleasure of updating the book and carrying on its tradition with the advice of William Beard and his daughter Arlene Beard.

DETLEV F. VAGTS
Professor of Law
Harvard University

Cambridge, Mass.
March 1989

CONTENTS

★★

INTRODUCTION   1

GEORGE WASHINGTON   9

JOHN ADAMS   13

THOMAS JEFFERSON   17

JAMES MADISON   21

JAMES MONROE   25

JOHN QUINCY ADAMS   29

ANDREW JACKSON   33

MARTIN VAN BUREN   37

WILLIAM HENRY HARRISON   41

JOHN TYLER   45

JAMES K. POLK   49

ZACHARY TAYLOR   53

MILLARD FILLMORE   57

FRANKLIN PIERCE   61

JAMES BUCHANAN   65

viii ★ CONTENTS ★

ABRAHAM LINCOLN 69
ANDREW JOHNSON 73
ULYSSES S. GRANT 77
RUTHERFORD B. HAYES 81
JAMES A. GARFIELD 85
CHESTER A. ARTHUR 89
GROVER CLEVELAND 93
BENJAMIN HARRISON 97
WILLIAM MCKINLEY 101
THEODORE ROOSEVELT 105
WILLIAM H. TAFT 109
WOODROW WILSON 113
WARREN G. HARDING 117
CALVIN COOLIDGE 121
HERBERT C. HOOVER 125
FRANKLIN D. ROOSEVELT 129
HARRY S. TRUMAN 137
DWIGHT D. EISENHOWER 143
JOHN F. KENNEDY 149
LYNDON B. JOHNSON 155
RICHARD M. NIXON 161
GERALD R. FORD 169
JAMES E. CARTER 173
RONALD W. REAGAN 179
GEORGE H. W. BUSH 185
BIOGRAPHICAL DIGEST 189

INTRODUCTION

★★

UNIVERSAL history, the history of what man has accomplished in this world," says Carlyle at one place, "is at bottom the History of the Great Men who have worked here." Yet this same Carlyle declared on another occasion that history is "a broad, deep Immensity, and each atom is 'chained' and completed with all." Roots of the living present, he added, "are with Father Adam himself and the cinders of Eve's first fire."

Here are two conceptions of history that have long been in contradiction. Carlyle was at war with himself in his own bosom over their meaning and truth. History is the story of great personalities; masses have merely stood and served. History is an immensity including billions of nameless and unknown men and women; the great personality is merely a drop in this tumultuous ocean tossing endlessly, through the ages; the mass movement is everything; the individual is an incident in it.

What is the truth of the business? Somewhere, I suspect, between the extremes. Certainly great personalities do not stand alone on a mountain or in a desert. They do not work in a vacuum. They live and do their work in times and places, with other men and women. They have meaning for us only in relation to the times, places, and humanity in which they live, act, and speak. Whatever they do, times and circumstances make it possible. With all the will in the world, George Washington as President could not have emancipated slaves by executive decree; nor could Lincoln, it seems, have escaped taking some action respecting slavery in his time and circumstances.

So close is the relation of the individual to mass movements that some historians are inclined to regard personalities as mere puppets performing actions and saying things made necessary by times and circumstances. Thus even the greatest of personalities are, in truth, as naught. They are cogs in a gear, turning with the immense machine called universal history.

Yet whoever inquires minutely into the history of personalities and their times cannot be so sure of such mechanics. Take, for example, the case of Lincoln. I have said above that Lincoln, "it seems," could not avoid doing something about slavery in the midst of the great Civil War. From all sides men and women were urging him to emancipate slaves. Day after day they bombarded him with petitions and even employed threats. But on the other side were high counsellors in his own administration who warned him against taking that step. No historian can find a mathematical formula for the outcome, such as, "Pressure for emancipation 12.3654, Pressure against emancipation 9.321; therefore, Lincoln had to issue the Proclamation of Emancipation." Besides Pressures there was the time element. Some decision had to be made respecting the day on which the act was to be performed. Here, too, no mathematical formula can be found, such as, on September 22, 1862, Pressure for emancipation reached 12.3654 which was the point at which action became necessary.

These formulas look absurd in the light of thousands of facts known about Lincoln and his times. They are absurd. Yet, if personalities are cogs in machines, without any independent will or power, the fact must be proved by some such very positive evidence. It simply cannot be done.

Within some hard limits of necessity each personality must work, but within these limits, which cannot be definitely fixed, the individual may make history, little or much. And personalities differ among themselves in respect of their desire, will, and ingenuity in making history. Many are content to drift with the stream. According to reports, Calvin Coolidge once said that he did not want to be a "great" President. If he really said it, he merely meant that he had no desire to effect important changes in the policies and measures of the government over which he presided. Yet to call his age prosperous and complacent does not fully explain his desires and purposes. There is not a time or place in which some immense change cannot be effected or at least set in the train of accomplishment.

On the other hand, there are times and circumstances which appear to compel great action. The banking and industrial crisis confronting Franklin D. Roosevelt on March 4, 1933, seemed to demand action on a large scale. To certain appearances, they did, judging by the stresses and strains of the day. Yet nearly a hundred years before that day, President Martin Van Buren confronted a banking and industrial crisis relatively as great, and simply refused to do anything significant about the exigencies of the hour. In the meantime, however, the thought of the American people changed in many respects. President Hoover had adopted several measures to combat the crisis. President Roosevelt extended these devices and added others. Still it is impossible now to discover in the changed circumstances and thought the "things" which determined the actions and policies of either President Hoover or President Roosevelt. There is, in truth, something original, something unique in each personality, and in the ages of history. No personality is ever repeated in history, and the idea that "History repeats itself" is a false and superficial view of history.

All we are warranted in saying, then, seems to be that the times help to make Presidents what they are and do, and that Presidents help to make their times. Personalities apart from times are meaningless myths. Times without personalities are shadows. Since the adoption of the Constitution, Presidents as personalities and American society in all its phases have evolved together. In time, one President succeeds another; society goes on in an unbroken stream.

Among the Presidents are some accounted "great" and others "small." Probably general consent could be found for the proposition that Washington, Jefferson, Jackson, and Lincoln were "great" Presidents, and Polk, Pierce, Fillmore, and Buchanan were lesser lights if not petty figures in history. Why are Washington, Jefferson, Jackson, and Lincoln accorded greatness? No exact answer is possible. But their position in popular appreciation is doubtless due, in some measure, to the fact that they lived and acted in times of social upheaval —when the American Revolution was in full blast, when democracy was launched, when the Civil War was raging.

Looked at closely, Lincoln seems to be in some respects a small man. His biographer, Albert J. Beveridge, once remarked to me in substance: "I wish I could discover how that petty politician of 1846 became the author of the Second Inaugural Address." Had Lincoln died in 1846, his biography would occupy scarcely ten lines in any dictionary, for he was to appearances a politician of small caliber. It is easy to say that "the times made him great," but that is not the whole answer. There were elements of singular power in Lincoln. Given opportunity they flowered into singular qualities of mind and spirit. Had Seward been chosen instead of Lincoln in 1860, Seward would not have been transformed into a Lincoln by the times, whatever the times might have made him do. Had Polk or

Pierce been in the White House in 1863, history would tell a different story of the one or the other, no doubt. And for aught we know, that story might display features of true grandeur. So little do we know of the causes of things.

Is the quality of our Presidents rising or declining? There are some students of history who feel competent to answer that question. Mr. Herbert Agar is among them. In his book called *The People's Choice* he declares that "one feature of a money-bossed democracy is that good men learn to refrain from public life....The early history of the Republic gives the example of a State served by its best men." Then he conveys the impression that, since the advent of Jacksonian democracy, the quality of the Presidents, with exceptions, has been below that of the early days and, on the whole, descending.

This is in effect an interpretation of all American history as well as the quality of Presidents. Has the Republic been running downhill since the days of the Fathers? An affirmative answer casts doubts on the Fathers also. They founded the Republic. They gave form to its government. They proclaimed its first ideals and set its traditions. They helped to prepare the generation that followed them. How did it happen that in their goodness and wisdom they brought forth a generation that knew not goodness and wisdom? How can anyone be called a great statesman if he leaves a heritage that comes soon to confusion?

Pessimism or optimism respecting the qualities of Presidents is not a matter of science, or knowledge, or reason. It is the outcome of a temperament and a social philosophy. To say that the Republic has been running downhill since the heroic age of the Fathers is to cry out against all history — nothing less than this. History is a mistake. It may be; but how does one know it? And who is the person who feels competent to know it?

There have been, it is true, in every period, philosophers of "the golden age," who love to look back and to make for themselves a mirage of an ideal past. That is, to some, a pleasing pastime. But so far as knowledge goes it is a mere pastime.

Is it true in these latter days, that "the best men" have refrained from public affairs? If so, by what right is a person called "best" when he refuses to do what appears to be a duty? Were the men who went into banking, industry, and stock speculation better men than the "politicians"? If so, how does anyone know it? By what criteria or measurements is the fact established? Were there in the American Republic between 1865 and 1933 men equal in "goodness" to the Fathers of the Republic? If there were such men and they deliberately refrained from public affairs do they deserve the title of "best"? Were there better men in 1884 than Cleveland, or in 1896 than McKinley? If so, who were they? If there were no men equal to the Fathers, then some fundamental defect has afflicted mankind in America. If we are running downhill, who are the saviors to turn the current and run us up again? Perhaps American history, in common with all history, is a mistake, a grand *faux pas*, but human wisdom is not equal to the task of proving it or disproving it.

Anyone who puts Washington, Hamilton, Jefferson, and John Adams under a high-powered microscope can, if he chooses, make them appear small men. Jefferson thought Hamilton a tool of plutocracy, and Hamilton regarded Jefferson as the archmaster of chicanery. Washington once complained that he had been treated like a common criminal and declared that Randolph was the worst liar on earth. He also expressed the opinion that Jefferson was an insincere man. Indeed if we pay serious attention to the remarks which party leaders have made about one another, we may well wonder whether any good statesmen ever lived at any period in American history. That leaders in public affairs in the early days were more disinterested and honorable than, let us say, Woodrow Wilson or Herbert Hoover, cannot be demonstrated. In cold truth, a good case could be made for the contrary proposition.

Measuring goodness and greatness is in fact hazardous business. Every person in practice symbolizes many qualities of human nature, if not all of them. He has his great moments and his hours of pettiness and meanness. None is a graven image all the time. It is because this is true that almost any character in history can be deified or debunked, according to the mood and intention of the biographer. After deification is completed, elements of human dross obtrude themselves upon the vision. After debunking is completed, some godlike qualities appear here and there. No person is as good or as bad as he or she can be, unless forsooth we take the fatalist view of all things. So knowledge of human nature and the charity born of caution suggest diffidence. Those who will judge may themselves be judged.

At all events, the Presidents, great and small, best and worst, are a part of American history. They have helped to make that history. They have expressed its qualities of character.

Whither are the Presidents and the Nation tending? Knowledge of the past does not enable us to predict the future with any degree of certainty. Such predictions as we choose to make will depend more upon our desires than our knowledge. Yet we may conclude with Carlyle: "Let us search more and more into the Past; let all men explore it, as the true fountain of knowledge; by whose light alone, consciously or unconsciously employed, can the Present and the Future be interpreted or guessed at."

CHARLES A. BEARD.

NEW MILFORD, CONN.

GEORGE WASHINGTON

★★★

LONG live George Washington, President of the United States!" With this cry the first Chief Magistrate of the Republic was greeted at the hour of his inauguration. The shout was taken up by the throng in front of Federal Hall, echoed through the streets of New York City and mingled with the roar of salutes on the Battery. Thus, on April 30, 1789, the Federal Government sanctioned by the Constitution, and then representing eleven states, was launched amid the rejoicings of the multitude at the Capital.

On that afternoon the weight of fifty-seven years lay heavily on Washington's shoulders—eventful, crowded years. It is true that his early days ran tranquilly, as he played in field and forest and gathered the rudiments of learning in a neighborhood school. But at the age of twenty-three as an officer in British service, on the scene of Braddock's defeat, his career of leadership began. There the young Virginian heard the whine of bullets, saw men falling to death around him, and tested the courage of his heart. Henceforth George Washington was a public man—of action.

He served in the Virginia legislature, where he showed stage-fright in making speeches but assurance in reaching decisions. From day to day, as he managed his plantation, he watched the growing tension between America and Great Britain. At last he threw himself upon the side of resistance, and was elected a member of the Continental Congress, made commander of the American forces at Cambridge, and entrusted with the military fate of the Revolution. For seven long years he was in the field—victorious at Boston, defeated on Long Island, harried down through New Jersey, imprisoned by winter at Valley Forge, and driven by unfailing will through to the end at Yorktown. Steadfastly refusing at any time to risk all on a single throw of the dice, though he was criticized for inaction and accused of timidity, Washington managed to hold the revolutionary army together and to inspire confidence in civilians until the struggle was brought to a triumphant finish.

When the war was over the victorious General surrendered his authority to the Congress and retired to his home at Mount Vernon. But he had scarcely returned to private life when the clash of civil strife broke in upon his peace. Rumors of popular rebellions, talk of monarchy, and scheming for military dictatorship arose and alarmed him. Washington then urged the formation of a stronger government, not by the scepter or the sword, but by discussion, proposition, and ratification. To this end he accepted membership in the constitutional convention of 1787, presided over its deliberations and acted as conciliator behind the scenes. His friends pressed him to lend the weight of his name and personality to the federal experiment agreed upon. So Washington accepted the presidency, and for eight years devoted his talents to civil administration as he had once employed them in war.

With skill in judging character, President Washington took care to install in power as members of the cabinet high officers, and judges, men loyal to the new economic order. Under his administration, the federal judicial system was created, arrangements were made to pay the revolutionary debts, a protective tariff was enacted, the first United States bank was established, and encouragement was given to commerce. When war broke out between France and Great Britain in 1793, Washington chose the neutral course in foreign affairs and warned his countrymen against entangling alliances. When domestic disputes over his measures grew bitter, when Hamilton and Jefferson quarreled, the President sought to effect a reconciliation. When this failed he leaned to the side of Hamilton only to be assailed by the barbed shafts of the opposition. That was too much. The endless recrimination wearied him; so he rejected a third term and retired again to Mount Vernon, with only two brief years of life before him. Death saved him from his design to plunge into the partisan fray against Jefferson a year later when the Federalists needed him. And George Washington was drawn into American tradition as the supreme patriot, above parties, above interests, above personalities, commanding the undivided sentiments of the nation.

John Adams

JOHN ADAMS

★★

A S BEFITTED the spirit of co-operation among the states
which marked the Constitution, the office of Chief
Executive passed in 1797 to John Adams, of Massachusetts. In
temper, thought, and experience the successor offered a contrast to Washington. Adams, though in his boyhood he had
hoed corn on his father's farm, received his education at Harvard. Young John Adams was poring over books, papers, and
lawyers' briefs while the youthful Washington was galloping
on horseback over his plantation. While Washington was serving the Revolution on the battlefield, Adams was upholding
the cause in the Continental Congress and as American agent
abroad—at The Hague and Paris. After peace came, he continued in office, accepting the uncomfortable post of minister
at the Court of George III, where he acquitted himself with
dignity, if not ingenuity.

Chosen Vice President in the first and second elections,
Adams took part in the negotiations, debates, and squabbles
which occurred during the eight years of Washington's administration. Then the mantle fell upon him in the election of
1796, but with an ominous dissent registered in a large opposition vote. In fact he was disliked by the Hamilton wing of the

13

Federalist party, to which he belonged, and was assailed by the Republicans who wanted to put Jefferson in his place. Hence Adams had few happy days in the executive chamber. Revolution was raging in France, war in Europe, and the interminable party dissension at home. The people were in no mood to accept any presidential decisions with unanimity—not even Adams' defiance of France for an alleged effort to levy tribute on the United States, known as the XYZ affair. In an attempt to bring about harmony, the Federalists rushed through Congress in 1798 the alien and sedition bills which laid heavy penalties on those who dared criticize the government. But instead of silencing critics these laws made Republicans madder than ever.

It is doubtful whether Washington himself could have ridden the storm. Certainly Adams did not. He toiled hard and earnestly, but by temper and conviction he was unfitted to quell a popular tumult. In his study of history he had acquired a deadly fear of the rich and the poor—plutocrat and proletarian; and in his philosophic writings on government he had issued warnings against the perils of rule by the people. Occupying the middle ground between plutocracy and democracy, Adams satisfied no extremists. In his campaign for re-election he was unjustly accused of being a monarchist at heart and rightly suspected of hostility to the political ideals incorporated in the Declaration of Independence. Popular reaction against "the aristocracy" was now running high, and without the prestige of Washington at their command, the Federalists were routed and driven from power. In the gray dawn of March 4, 1801, John Adams rode away from the Capital that his eyes might not behold the inauguration of the triumphant Jefferson.

THOMAS JEFFERSON

★★

L IKE the first President, the third Chief Executive, Thomas Jefferson, was a son of Virginia, a planter, and a slave-owner. But he was a civilian, a reformer, not a soldier. With truth it could be said that he was the most highly civilized man ever called to the presidency. Educated at William and Mary College, interested in science, education, philosophy, art, archi-tecture, and music, as well as public affairs, he was broader in learning and wider in outlook than either Washington or Adams. During the American Revolution and the subsequent years, he had labored in his study and at the council table—as governor of Virginia, member of the state legislature, repre-sentative of the Old Dominion in the Continental Congress, minister to France, and Secretary of State under Washington. The Declaration of Independence was drafted by his hand; in Virginia he led the attack on the landed aristocracy which abolished primogeniture, or inheritance by the eldest son, and forced the division of great estates, and there he also pushed through a bill establishing religious liberty. Jefferson stood forth as the fearless champion of human rights, of religious freedom, and of liberty of press and speech.

When President Washington called him home from his

diplomatic post in France to serve as Secretary of State, Jefferson was drawn into the domestic conflict over Hamilton's policies. He had not been in America while the Constitution was being drafted and he was somewhat bewildered at first by the political storm; but he went along with his colleague, Hamilton, in the Treasury Department. At length convinced that Hamilton was building up a financial oligarchy at the expense of farmers and planters, Jefferson opposed the creation of the United States Bank. When the war broke out in Europe and the French revolution took an extreme course, Jefferson's sympathies were with France and the revolutionists. Thus to differences with Hamilton over domestic affairs were added differences over foreign policy—and he found Washington on Hamilton's side in fact, if conciliatory in spirit. Jefferson resigned as Secretary of State, rode home to Virginia, and opened a campaign to drive out of power the Federalists and their leader, the Secretary of the Treasury.

Possessing no oratorical talents, Jefferson did not take the stump. He resorted to negotiations instead. With a facile mind, he carried on his operations mainly by writing letters and consulting with friends—by methods which his enemies called "intrigues." He avoided direct attacks on Washington, and cleverly turned Hamilton's decisions and policies to partisan account. Before long the ground swell of popular demand for Jefferson's leadership became apparent. It was so strong by 1796 that he stood second to John Adams in the electoral vote and won for himself the office of Vice President. Four years later Jefferson was swept into the White House by a domestic upheaval called at the time "the great revolution." As yet his party was merely Republican in name, but it was already tinctured with the spirit of democracy so feared by the framers of the Constitution.

His two terms in office were filled with turmoil—wars in Europe and economic distresses at home. Hating the brazen clangor of arms, Jefferson resolved to keep the peace. Rather than throw the country into the maelstrom of war, he resorted to embargoes on shipping and to endless negotiations with Great Britain and Napoleon. Few were wholly satisfied with his administration; neither the "hawks" clamoring for a war of vengeance and conquest against Great Britain, nor the Yankee shippers clamoring for the right to sell freely to belligerents. At the end of his second term, heartily sick of politics, Jefferson welcomed escape and literally fled to Virginia, leaving "the hornets' nest" to his Secretary of State, James Madison.

Three great achievements could be ascribed to his administration: the purchase of the Louisiana territory, the Lewis and Clark expedition to the Pacific Ocean, and the beginning of the National Road uniting the seaboard with the Mississippi Valley. Yet it was not for these things that he most desired to be remembered. To direct the judgment of posterity he wrote the epitaph for his own monument: "Author of the Declaration of American Independence, of the Statute of Virginia for Religious Freedom, and Father of the University of Virginia." Such was his verdict on his work.

Although freed from official responsibility in 1809, Jefferson continued to be the quiet counselor of Madison and Monroe, amid days crowded with study, correspondence, and conversation. He became reconciled at last with his old adversary, John Adams; and the aged two men exchanged views on themes high and wide until death carried them off dramatically on the same day, July 4, 1826.

James Madison

JAMES MADISON

★★

U NDER James Madison the Virginia dynasty was continued in the office of President. He was of the civilian
school to which Jefferson belonged: a graduate of Princeton,
a student of history, and inquirer into the arts of government.
While Washington and Hamilton had faced steel on the battlefield, Madison had served in council chamber, in the Virginia
legislature and the Continental Congress. He early took part
in the movement for a stronger union which eventuated in the
constitutional convention. He helped to draw up a new plan
of government, toiled assiduously as a delegate at the convention, stamped his political philosophy upon its thought, made
careful notes of the proceedings, and as a member of the first
Congress aided in putting the Federal Government to work.
For eight years he served Jefferson as Secretary of State. Yet
he was, strictly speaking, no politician. Madison was above all
a social philosopher. He saw deeply into the motives of mankind, especially the economic motives. Exploring the past he
discovered class conflicts everywhere. Looking forward into
the future, he beheld with troubled spirit a time when American society would be torn by struggles between owners of
property and the "indigent" masses. Small in stature, mild in

manner, diffident and introspective, he was poorly equipped for the rough and tumble of politics.

For eight tumultuous years this scholar-philosopher held the presidency. This man of peace, without Jefferson's resolve, was finally drawn into war. British vessels were searching American ships, the French preyed on American commerce, Madison's difficulties multiplied. Some critics cried for war on France, others for war on Britain, and still others, few in number, for peace. In the end, Madison was overborne by the "war hawks," under John C. Calhoun and Henry Clay, and was driven into the second conflict with England. Thus he was compelled to preside over a struggle which brought, instead of tangible gains, a staggering debt, a disordered currency, and the destruction of the Capitol. Although Andrew Jackson's victory at New Orleans provided glory for patriots, the war, in cold truth, closed with a treaty by which the United States gained none of the concessions for which it had ostensibly fought. And to cap the climax, Madison witnessed the restoration, by his party, of the economic system once sponsored by Alexander Hamilton and assailed by Jefferson—a second United States Bank, a protective tariff, and a huge funded debt. With a sigh of relief, this war President in his turn retired to Virginia in 1817—to study, to speculate on man's destiny, and to advise James Monroe, his successor, unobtrusively. Living to the ripe old age of eighty-five, Madison—"The Father of the Constitution"—witnessed the defiance of the Union by South Carolina, and heard the distant rumble of the impending civil conflict.

James Monroe

JAMES MONROE

★★

W ITH the inauguration of James Monroe in 1817, the generation of the American Revolution made its farewell bow. Monroe had been a soldier of the War for Independence, wounded in action, and tried by fire. In mentality and outlook he was more akin to Washington than to Jefferson or Madison. He had been educated at William and Mary and trained in law, but he did not have the philosophic grasp of Madison or the wide human sympathies of Jefferson. He had, it is true, seen long public service—in the Virginia legislature, in the Continental Congress, as United States Senator, as representative of the Government in England, France, and Spain, as Secretary of State, and Secretary of War under Madison. But this service had been solid and prosaic rather than dramatic and brilliant. The presidency had come to him through the influence of Jefferson and Madison and political maneuvering, not because he fascinated the public and awakened great popular enthusiasm.

Monroe's eight years in power were marked by four events which made his administration memorable. The first was the great business panic that broke in 1819—and shook the economic structure of western civilization, foreshadowing similar disturbances in the capitalist system. The following year (1820-21), with Monroe's approval, Congress effected the famous Missouri Compromise between slavery and freedom. By its terms each side won something: Missouri was admitted to the Union as a slave state and Maine as a free state; while the remaining Louisiana territory was divided into free and slave regions by the parallel of 36° 30'.

In 1821 Monroe brought to a conclusion negotiations with Spain, adding Florida to the territorial heritage of the American nation. Then, in 1823, confronted by the possibility of European intervention in the western hemisphere, Monroe expounded, in a message to Congress, the doctrine that now bears his name. In prolix language, he warned the Old World that the United States would regard as unfriendly any European interference with independent countries in the New World, and would not tolerate new colonization or the seizure of more territory in the two Americas.

Having added this postscript to Jefferson's Declaration of Independence, Monroe rested on his laurels and withdrew from his high office in 1825 more content with fate, perhaps, than the distinguished Virginians who had preceded him into retirement.

J. Q. Adams

JOHN QUINCY ADAMS

★★★

BY A STRANGE turn in the kaleidoscope of history, the
presidency of the United States fell, on March 4, 1825,
to John Quincy Adams, son of John Adams. The father had
been humiliated and driven from power by the Republicans.
In mid-stream the son had left his father's party, had joined
the Jeffersonians, had been denounced by the Federalists, and
had accepted office under a Republican administration. Now
the father beheld the son rise to the high eminence on which
his ambitions had once been centered. With what mixed feel-
ings he must have contemplated the changes in manners and
fortunes!

Yet the consolation which John Adams gathered from the
occasion was not unalloyed, for his son had not won a majority
of the popular ballots or the electoral votes. Andrew Jackson
stood first; but by astute manipulations in the House of Representatives, where the election was thrown, under the Constitution, John Quincy Adams had been made Chief Executive.
Nothing that he had done or afterward accomplished could
overcome the mishap that accompanied his rise to the presidency. Compared with Jackson, he was an unpopular leader.
He had been educated at Harvard and in Europe—not on the

frontier whence new heroes were to come—and he was a dour, reserved, dogmatic man, with a puritan conscience. To be sure, he had served his country well as minister to Holland, Portugal, Prussia, and Russia. To be sure also, he had labored hard as Monroe's Secretary of State, contributing to the formulation of the Monroe Doctrine. But there was nothing about him to attract wide sympathy in an age when frontier democracy was flooding into Washington, athirst for power and office.

In many ways Adams was ahead of his time. He wanted to exclude mere job hunters from the public service, to conserve natural resources, to promote science and the arts, to launch great public improvements, and to keep the public lands, as a kind of national treasury, out of the hands of "land hungry wolves." With sad foreboding he saw the outcome of the slavery contest that was beginning to rage, and would have mitigated its violence. But everything was against him. His opponents in Congress riddled his plans. Politicians in his own official family undermined him. If any noteworthy measure is to be associated with his administration it is the highly protective Tariff Act known as the Tariff of Abominations, which almost made a revolution in South Carolina. At the end of a single term he was routed by the Jacksonians. Staggered by the blow for a moment, Adams returned to public life as a humble member of the House of Representatives. There the "old man eloquent" slaved at his duties until 1848, and linked his name forever with civil liberty by a valiant defense of the right of the people to petition Congress for a redress of grievances.

ANDREW JACKSON

★★★

IN THE personality and administration of Andrew Jackson—"Old Hickory of Tennessee"—economic and social changes, long in process, came to full political expression. Planting and farming had spread to the Mississippi and beyond. Machine industries with their armies of wage earners and urban "mobs" so feared by Jefferson were swiftly overturning the economy of the handloom and oxcart in the Northeast. Besides Vermont and Maine nine new western states, predominantly agricultural, had been admitted to the Union, with manhood suffrage or liberal qualifications on the right to vote in their constitutions. As the Federalist party declined, Eastern states had broken down property restraints on voting and given the ballot to nearly every white man. In short, a democracy of farmers and mechanics had arrived on the political stage, clamoring for a share of the public offices. Evangelical revivalism in the backwoods had added religious zeal to political fervor. With the widening of the suffrage the choice of presidential electors was taken from state legislatures and vested in voters at the polls. The selection of candidates for President was wrested from compact groups of manipulators in Congress, known as the congressional caucus. For this inner cabal was substituted the national nominating convention, "fresh from the people," crowded with officeholders, and run by another inner cabal.

This transformation Jackson symbolized. All the Presidents before him had come from families of independent means. Five had been college graduates. All knew how to wear knee breeches, ruffles, and silver buckles, with grace. Jackson, on the other hand, was the son of a poor, struggling farmer on the border between the Carolinas, probably on the southern side of the line. Orphaned in boyhood, he had risen by his wits, talents, fists, and pistols to wealth and position. After a brief study of law in the office of an attorney in North Carolina, he had gone into Tennessee. There he served as prosecuting attorney, member of the state constitutional convention, Representative and Senator in the Congress of the United States, and commander of the state militia. Combining storekeeping, planting, and real estate speculation with politics, he amassed a fortune and acquired social position as a slave-owning planter, thus joining the economic class to which Washington, Jefferson, Madison and Monroe had belonged.

As head of the local militia Jackson spread terror among the Indians in border conflicts, while he endeared himself to his men by sharing their hardships. As commander of American forces at New Orleans in the War of 1812, he administered a smashing defeat to British regulars, thus adding "glory" to a conflict that had been marked by national humiliation. His love of horse races, cock fights, brawls, and duelling, won him an unquestioned reputation for personal courage. Although illiterate and quarrelsome, irascible and vengeful, he could be dignified on occasion and tender with friends who did not challenge him. He possessed the vaguest of vague ideas on such issues as the tariff, internal improvements, and public finance, and he could be quoted on either side of nearly any issue with assurance.

This people's war hero was swept into the office of President on the democratic tide and ruled with an iron hand for eight years, under the guidance of managers astute in the manufacture of publicity and the distribution of jobs and offices as political spoils. Coming in on a storm, he went out on a storm, with two positive achievements to his credit, one dubious, the other prophetic. He attacked and then destroyed the second United States Bank which he regarded as the corrupt engine of Eastern plutocracy. In its place he left a large number of state banks, many of which issued worthless paper money. When South Carolina defied the government by threatening to nullify federal law, he shouted that "the Union must be preserved" and threatened the use of force, while he helped to engineer a compromise that the Carolinians could call a victory for themselves. Amid the cheers and tears of his followers he retired from the White House to his plantation in Tennessee and received pilgrimages of the faithful until his death in 1845.

MARTIN VAN BUREN

★★

AT THE close of his second term in 1837 Jackson bequeathed his office to another son of the people, Martin Van Buren, offspring of a Dutch tavern keeper and farmer at Kinderhook, on a high road between Albany and New York City. As a barboy serving drinks to politicians who stopped at his father's inn, Martin received an early training in practical politics by listening to the lively debates of his elders. He took up the practice of law in New York City and made money while he built up a band of faithful followers among the braves of Tammany Hall. Soon he climbed from office to office, outwitting and bewildering alike old Federalists and opponents in his own party, now boldly called "Democratic" instead of "Republican." In succession he was Attorney General of New York, state senator, United States Senator, governor, Secretary of State under Jackson, minister to Great Britain, and Vice President during Jackson's last term.

Small in stature, smooth in manner, a bit foppish, above all adroit, Van Buren captivated the Hero of New Orleans. He was not an orator or a writer. If called upon for a clear-cut answer on a public question, he could reply with a stream of words that dumbfounded the questioner. He did not seek to overwhelm by thunder. Rightly he was called "the Red Fox." With truth it was said that Van Buren always rowed toward his object "with muffled oars." He made politics a trade, using the spoils of office as the bait to capture followers. He was, in fact, the chief architect of machine politics—the use of government jobs, favors, and contracts to weld party directors into a compact mass, to reward friends and punish foes. Though he vociferously championed the people, his name cannot be correctly associated with a single measure of popular beneficence. A late biographer can only say for him that he stood staunchly against giving federal aid to industry, agriculture, and labor laid prostrate by the panic of 1837, and that he proposed to separate the Federal Treasury from banking. Dexterous as he was, however, Van Buren was retired at the end of one term; and, despite twisting and turning, despite flirtation with the anti-slavery minority, he could never recover the throne.

W. H. Harrison

WILLIAM HENRY HARRISON

★★★

B
Y 1840 the Democrats, under Jackson's leadership, had
broken away from the symbols of politics—protective
tariffs, centralized banking, and special favors for business—
which had been accepted by the Republicans at the close of
the second war with Great Britain (See p. 22). By that year
also old Federalists and younger men of their school, who had
sulked in their tents, were hard at work building up an opposition to nearly all that Jackson stood for. The era of good feeling under Republican auspices had come to an end. The
National Republican party, later called Whig, had come into
existence. But unable to get far with Daniel Webster, "the
merchants' pet," or with Henry Clay, open sponsor of the
unpopular United States Bank, the directors of the new party
took a leaf from the book of Jackson and Van Buren. No man
clearly associated in the public mind with "the interests" could
be elected in an age when farmers and mechanics had to be
cajoled and won over. So in 1840 the Whigs went into the new
West for a candidate and found William Henry Harrison.

From early manhood, Harrison had been an officeholder or
an office seeker. Son of Benjamin Harrison (a signer of the
Declaration of Independence), educated at Hampden Sydney

College in Virginia, William Henry had cast in his lot with the West. He had been secretary of the Northwest Territory, a Representative and Senator in the Congress of the United States, and minister to Colombia. Still more to the point of popular politics, he had defeated Indians at the battle of Tippecanoe and had commanded American troops in the War of 1812. In the evening of life he resided in a comfortable house in Ohio—a house with a log wing.

Here was the man for the Whig directors—a military hero and a log cabin farmer, whose ideas on political issues were nebulous. The only problem, as the former head of the defunct United States Bank, Nicholas Biddle, put it, was to keep Harrison from saying or writing anything on the issues of the day. In a whirlwind campaign, based on the appeal of log cabins, hard cider, coon-skins, and military glory, the Whigs outwitted Van Buren and put Harrison into the White House. But, alas for designs, Harrison survived the ordeal for only one month, and dying, left his high office to John Tyler, the Vice President, on April 4, 1841.

John Tyler

JOHN TYLER

★★

IT WAS a sad day for the Whigs when John Tyler became Chief Executive, for he was a stranger in their midst. He had been a Jeffersonian Republican, a member of the Virginia legislature, governor of the Old Dominion, and a United States Senator. A graduate of William and Mary College, he had been chosen rector and chancellor of that institution. In all things Tyler was conservative. With the Whig directorate in the North he had little or no sympathy. He had, it is true, run on a Whig ticket for Vice President in 1836, but principally as a states' rights advocate, because he disliked the strong nationalism of Jacksonian Democracy. Four years later he had been associated with Harrison for the purpose of catching Southern votes, and so it was a case of the biter bitten.

Once installed in the White House Tyler spent the remainder of his single term in unhappy conflicts with both Whigs and Democrats in Congress. Little that he suggested in the way of legislation was acceptable to them, and little that they desired was pleasing to him. He did manage to put through a treaty with Great Britain settling the northeastern boundary of the United States and a treaty with China opening ports of trade. These measures, satisfactory enough to Whigs, he crowned in the last months of his administration by sponsoring a joint resolution of Congress for the annexation of Texas, another slave state. Thus he stirred up an anti-slavery storm while preparing the way for a war with Mexico. Brushed rudely aside in the election of 1844, Tyler returned to Virginia, where he continued his advocacy of states' rights; and when the break came in 1861 he was elected a member of the Confederate Congress. Had death not carried him off, his last services would have been to "the lost cause."

JAMES K. POLK

★★★

WITH no other military hero like Harrison available in
1844, the Whigs nominated Henry Clay, despite the
continued popular distrust of the man who had led in the
struggle to re-establish the United States Bank. The Democrats
were in a similar plight. Remembering what had happened to
Martin Van Buren four years before, they cast him off, although he was maneuvering for the place with all his old
adroitness. Deprived of the prize himself, "the Red Fox" of
Kinderhook promoted the selection of James K. Polk, as a
"dark horse" candidate. In some respects, however, Polk had
the marks of "availability." He was the son of a North Carolina
farmer. Though educated at the University of that state, he
had gone to the frontier of Tennessee and practiced law, as an
active Democrat, among the farmers and planters of Jackson's
section. Polk had quickly won for himself the title of "Napoleon of the stump," and had been elected to the state legislature, to the office of governor, and finally to the House of
Representatives in Washington. He was thus not unknown to
politics, but nobody could find any reasons for calling him
famous. Appealing to popular passions by promising "the Re-

annexation of Texas," and threatening Great Britain with a war over the Oregon boundary, Polk carried the day.

Since Texas had been annexed under Tyler, Polk sent troops into territory claimed by Mexico, where they came into collision with Mexican soldiers. Then he was able to announce that "war exists by act of Mexico" and to rally the country in support of a struggle that ended in victory and the addition of a vast domain in the Southwest. His dispute with Great Britain over the Oregon boundary Polk settled without securing the "fifty-four, forty" parallel or fighting—indeed by accepting a compromise line far south of the points so vociferously claimed. In the war, however, he raised up a Whig military hero, Zachary Taylor, who was to turn the Democrats out of power in the next election. Having declared himself in favor of one term for President and having found out that he could not win the renomination anyway, Polk graciously stepped aside in 1848 and then retired the following year to Tennessee where death overtook him in a few months.

Zachary Taylor

ZACHARY TAYLOR

★★

IT WAS a unique figure that entered the White House on March 4, 1849—Zachary Taylor, the last of the planters to possess the presidency. Taylor had been exalted as a military hero, but unlike Jackson and Harrison before him he had not seen long service in state and federal positions before his election. The son of an army officer, he had entered the army at the age of twenty-three. He had drifted into Louisiana, and there managed to get possession of a large plantation and a drove of slaves. Besides attending to his estate, he fought Indians on the frontier, and then, in the Mexican war, he caught popular imagination as the victor at Buena Vista. This triumph was meat for the Whigs. Clay and Webster had publicly committed themselves in favor of commerce, banking, and industry. They were marked men. But General Taylor had no bitter foes. In politics moderation was his strong point; he declared that he was "a Whig, but not an ultra Whig." Touching the chief economic issues then being debated he said: "On the subjects of the tariff, the currency, and the improvement of our great highways, the will of the people as expressed by their representatives in Congress ought to be respected and carried out by the executive." Nominated by the Whigs on this vague declaration of faith, Taylor defeated the Democrats; but he died in 1850, before he could give effect to any program, if he had ever thought of one.

Millard Fillmore

MILLARD FILLMORE

★★★

T AYLOR'S unfinished term fell to the Vice President,
Millard Fillmore. Fillmore was the son of a farmer, born
in a log cabin in western New York, and he had used the
familiar "log cabin" issue in the campaign in 1848. Meagerly
educated, he had worked his way upward through school-
teaching to the practice of law in Buffalo. Some political experience he had garnered in the state legislature and in the
House of Representatives at Washington. On one public question he had been outspoken: he was opposed to slavery and
the extension of this "peculiar institution" into the territories.
It was this record which the Whigs employed in the North to
offset the pro-slavery sympathies of his companion, General
Taylor, the Louisiana planter. But when the presidency came
to him as a stroke of fortune, Fillmore lent his support to the
Great Compromise of 1850 with its harsh act for the recapture
of fugitive slaves. In this way he alienated the anti-slavery
party of the North. Although Southern Whigs rallied around
him in the nominating convention of 1852, Fillmore could not
gain sufficient strength among Northern delegates to win the
coveted place on the ballot. So in 1853 he went back to his
home, where for many years he sought to be a model citizen,

as a biographer says, "taking the deepest interest in the civil, religious, and intellectual development of the community." Apart from the Great Compromise of 1850, two measures were associated with his administration: Commodore Perry was dispatched to open trade with Japan and cheap postage was introduced; but neither of them can be ascribed to his initiative.

FRANKLIN PIERCE

★★★

O F THE two generals offered to the suffrage of the people
in 1852, Winfield Scott for the Whigs, and Franklin
Pierce for the Democrats, the latter was the lesser star in the
military firmament. Pierce had served acceptably in the war
against Mexico and had been injured when thrown from his
horse on the battlefield, but his renown did not rival that of
his chief, General Scott. In the arts of politics, however, he
was more of an adept. While Scott took the stump clumsily,
Pierce relied upon negotiations in the established custom of
Martin Van Buren.

Moreover, Pierce had been educated in the business of politics. His father, a New Hampshire farmer, had been an officer
in the Revolution and governor of the state. Pierce was to the
manner born. From Bowdoin College, he turned to the practice
of law, and found leisure for public affairs. His handsome
appearance, skillful oratory, and genial conversation helped
him forward rapidly—to the state legislature, the House of
Representatives, and the Senate of the United States. Yet in
1852, despite his military record, Pierce was a dark horse in
the national field. Other Democrats outranked him. At the
nominating convention it was only on the thirty-fifth ballot

that he appeared in the lists, with fifteen votes from Virginia; and it was only on the forty-ninth ballot that his backers carried the day. "A Northern man with Southern principles," he appealed to the South; a champion of religious liberty, he was a favorite with the Irish members of Tammany Hall. To crown it all, his friend, Nathaniel Hawthorne, wrote Pierce's campaign biography; and was rewarded with an office for his pains.

In the White House, President Pierce stood for two propositions pleasing to planters: anti-slavery agitation must be condemned and the tariff should be lowered. With his program for laying the slavery question to rest, only events quarreled. Democratic ministers to Great Britain, France, and Spain issued a manifesto calling for the seizure of Cuba—which would have meant another slave state; and Congress under the leadership of Stephen A. Douglas, in 1854, repealed the Missouri Compromise (See p. 26), and threw open to slavery all the territories of the West. Then popular protests against "the slave power" grew louder than ever. Then the Democrats looked for a candidate whose "Southern principles" were not so clear-cut, found him in James Buchanan, of Pennsylvania, and sent Pierce back to the green hills of New Hampshire.

James Buchanan

JAMES BUCHANAN

★★★

THE election returns in 1856 were ominous. A new party,
bearing the name of Jefferson's old organization, Republican, had entered the lists—against slavery in the territories;
and the combined vote of the Whigs and Republicans was
nearly half a million more than that cast for Buchanan. But
the future was unknown to the actors, and the Democrats
under Buchanan gave attention to matters immediately in front
of them. By throwing favors to Whigs they made a material
reduction in the tariff, and they withdrew subsidies from
American shipping. They allowed wildcat banking (See p. 35)
to go on undisturbed, and otherwise gave distress to businessmen. The anti-slavery faction they alarmed still more by
trying to bring Kansas into the Union as a slave state. And as
if to settle this troublesome question forever, the Supreme
Court of the United States, then under Democratic auspices,
decided in the Dred Scott case that Congress had no power to
abolish slavery in the territories. In short, Congress could
not interfere with this peculiar institution anywhere. Since
slavery could not be controlled under the Constitution by
peaceful processes, and agitation seemed to bear little fruit,
one John Brown took the law into his own hands and tried to

make a servile insurrection in Virginia—for which he paid with his own life.

During these tempestuous days from 1857 to 1861, James Buchanan pitched and tossed, growing more irritable from day to day, as he gave his support mainly to pro-slavery extremists. Rare insight and rare courage were needed, and Buchanan had neither. All his life he had been a politician gliding happily from office to office—as member of the Pennsylvania legislature, Representative in Congress, minister to Russia, United States Senator, Secretary of State, and minister to England. Now a merciless agitation over slavery, foreign to the customary conflicts over spoils, was wresting affairs out of the hands of old-line politicians, such as Buchanan was. In 1860 he was coldly pushed into the background. When Southern states began to secede from the Union, Buchanan wrung his hands, said his prayers on state affairs, and longed for the end of his hectic days in an office where he had little power, and yet was subjected to the burden of responsibility. He adhered to the negative course, was abused by both sides for making no positive decisions, and left the raging turmoil to Abraham Lincoln, to whom the presidency had been entrusted by the election of 1860.

Your friend as ever

A. Lincoln

ABRAHAM LINCOLN

★★

THE Chief Magistrate called to preside over a divided country in 1861 was the leader of the new Republican party which had made its appearance in the national campaign of 1856 in opposition to slavery in the territories. At its next convention it was strengthened by the addition of many Whigs who deserted the old ship. At the same time its economic program was widened. To the exclusion of slavery from the territories, it added an endorsement of the protective tariff and of the long-debated project for giving away the public lands, as homesteads, to farmers and laborers. In the states where slavery existed that labor system was not to be disturbed, but it was to be excluded from the territories of the Great West. As the platform was read to the Republican convention in 1860 the free-soil plank was applauded, and the tariff and homestead clauses were greeted by vociferous and prolonged cheers.

Given this platform, Abraham Lincoln was a strategic choice as presidential candidate. Lincoln could appeal to voters in the old stronghold of Jacksonian Democracy as the son of a poor farmer, born in Kentucky in 1809, reared in Indiana and Illinois, accustomed to hard labor in field and forest. He belonged to the humble tradition of the log cabin, which had been used with great effect in many campaigns. He was far removed from the culture of rich Whigs and rich planters— literally one of the plain people, to whom all politicians after Jackson had paid high tribute. He had hoed corn, split rails, boated on the Mississippi, kept a general store, practiced law on the frontier, told stories, and joked with hunters, farmers, and day laborers. His versatility in the game of small politics was beyond question. Years in the Illinois legislature he had supplemented by one term in the House of Representatives at Washington. If by no means as adroit as Van Buren, Lincoln knew the art of making trades and apportioning the spoils of office.

Yet despite the lowliness of his origin and the uncouthness of his body, there was something in the thought and spirit of Lincoln which differentiated him from the illiterate Andrew Jackson on the one side and the college-trained Pierce and Buchanan on the other. Denied all formal education, save a few months at a rude frontier school, Lincoln educated himself by studying humane letters—the New Testament, Aesop's Fables, the poetry of Robert Burns, and the tragedies of Shakespeare. Though fond of jokes, and skeptical in religion, he could brood with the saints of the ages, while he outwitted clever politicians in playing their game. With the economics of the Whig creed, he mingled the principles of equal rights drawn in part from the theories of Thomas Jefferson. Although willing to compromise with slavery as a vested interest in the states where it was sanctioned by law, Lincoln was opposed by deep sentiment to the institution and was determined to keep it out of the territories.

To this politician and dreamer fell the lot of guiding the North through the long Civil War. With his name will be forever associated one act of high resolve—the Proclamation emancipating slaves in the places in arms against the Union—

and the thirteenth amendment abolishing slavery throughout the United States. The first stroke, it has been said, was a war measure made necessary by the growing abolitionist agitation and by the demands of the armed conflict. Certainly without these pressures it would have been an empty gesture. But the necessity of emancipation cannot be proved. It may be contended with equal reason that the act sprang from the deep humanism of the Emancipator, who rose above circumstances in making use of them and expressing his will.

His judgment may have been far from unerring in the conduct of civil and military administration, but the abolition of slavery alone, sealed by the force of arms, was enough to assure Lincoln's immortality in the American democratic tradition. By his tragic death in the hour of triumph, the dross of his personality was burned away and he was spared the loss of majesty that would have come if he had lived through the storms of reconstruction, the struggle over the rights of Negroes, and the scandals that followed the close of the War. Even were emancipation forgotten, Lincoln's Gettysburg Address and Second Inaugural Address would remain imperishable among the classics of the written word, among the world's great declarations of faith and understanding.

ANDREW JOHNSON

★★

O N APRIL 14, 1865, executive power was transferred to the Vice President, Andrew Johnson, who had been associated with Lincoln in the election of the previous year. At that time, Republicans had cast aside their original name, called themselves the Union party, and sought to bring about a fusion of energies in the struggle for victory on the battle-field. For this purpose they had selected for Vice President a tried and true Jacksonian Democrat, Andrew Johnson. In origin and early experience, he was as humble as Jackson or Lincoln—the son of a porter and a maid employed at a tavern in Raleigh, North Carolina, apprenticed at the age of ten to a tailor. Irked by the harsh servitude imposed on him, he fled to a frontier town in Tennessee, where he soon learned to com-bine politics with cutting and sewing in a village tailor shop. His wife taught him to write. A local politician trained him in public affairs, and Johnson made his way from office to office. Before he had been nominated for the Vice Presidency, he had been alderman, mayor, member of the state legislature, Repre-sentative in Congress, United States Senator, and military governor of his state.

From first to last Johnson was loyal to the democracy of

small farmers. He was opposed to the United States Bank, and "the money power" affiliated with it. He was among the first to demand the distribution of public lands as homesteads. In Congress he denounced the protective tariff and internal improvements; and as governor of his state, he pleaded for public schools and the popular election of United States Senators. As a slave owner he had a certain tenderness for the Southern cause, despite his antipathy to the planting class.

Given this background, President Johnson was bound to come into collision with the Republican directors in Congress. They raised the protective tariff, set up a new national banking system, taxed state bank notes (See p. 35) out of existence, and adopted other economic measures contrary to the Jacksonian faith. Over reconstruction in the South, the spoils of office, and nearly everything else, President Johnson differed from the "radical" Republicans. He opposed giving freedmen the full right to vote at once and holding down the Southern whites by Northern bayonets. In anger Republicans induced the House of Representatives to impeach him before the Senate as a high court and it was only by a narrow margin that he escaped conviction and expulsion from the presidency. Powerful political factions in the Republican party rejected him, the Democrats—his former associates—discarded him; Johnson sank into the shadows of American history, from which he was not rescued by a competent biographer, Lloyd Paul Stryker, until the third decade of the twentieth century—just in time to be assailed anew by a champion of Negro rights, W. E. Burghardt Du Bois.

ULYSSES S. GRANT

★★

A WARE that they had commanded only a minority of the
popular vote in the country in the three previous elections, Republican managers in 1868 faced the necessity of
strengthening their position. If they were to uphold the laws
enacted during the War, put into effect their plans for the
reconstruction of the former confederate states, and maintain
their supremacy, they needed a candidate for President whose
popular appeal was beyond question. This candidate they
found in General Ulysses S. Grant. It was true that he had
voted the Democratic ticket in 1856 and had never cast a ballot for the Republicans. But he was available in ways beyond
enumeration. Born in Ohio, he was from the Valley of Democracy. The son of a farmer and tanner, he was in origin almost
humble enough to rank with Jackson, Lincoln, and Johnson.
A graduate of West Point, he had served loyally in the Mexican War, even though his heart was not in it. Resigning from
the Army in 1854, he had tried farming, the real estate business, and storekeeping, without success, and was running
downhill when he was lifted from oblivion by the outbreak
of the Civil War. From the colonelcy of an Illinois regiment,
he mounted swiftly through military achievements at Fort

Donelson, Vicksburg, and Chattanooga. Made Lieutenant General in 1864, he carried on the pitiless drive that ended at Appomattox and in the hour of victory he had been generous.

Though rather innocent in matters of politics, Grant was chosen as the Republican leader, given two terms in the White House, and plagued by a passion for a third term. For eight troubled years, full of struggles over reconstruction and the distresses of a financial panic, he hugely enjoyed the panoply of office. He was uncertain in many matters, but determined in two: paper money must be made payable in gold and Santo Domingo must be annexed as a home for Negroes and, as he said, an opportunity for "United States capitalists." In the routine of administration, he was victimized by friends, beset by scandals, and betrayed by spoilsmen. Reconstruction in the South, even if carried out with utmost prudence and conciliation, would have filled Grant's days with trials. As actually managed it thrust upon him perplexities beyond his powers. If he knew what went on in his administration, he was lacking in standards of propriety. A more charitable interpretation is that this bluff soldier, unaccustomed in his youth to riches and glory, was dazed as he wandered in the wonderland of post-war politics and dined among plutocrats bent on plunder. At the end, when the General wrote his classic memoirs while wrestling with the agony of death, the politician was forgotten and the soldier was remembered.

Sincerely
R. B. Hayes

RUTHERFORD B. HAYES

★★★

THAT the Republican party, which had come to power as a minority in 1860, was losing its grip became evident in the congressional elections of 1874 when the Democrats captured the House of Representatives. The country was tossing in the distress of a business depression, accompanied by strikes and disorders that frightened the possessors of good things. A third party was rearing its head, to the alarm of old political managers. Scandals in the Grant administration had shocked even loyal supporters of the man who had saved the Republic on the battlefield. The leading aspirant for the Republican nomination, James G. Blaine, had been, rightly or wrongly, associated in the public mind with some of the worst peculations.

In the circumstances, the Republicans resorted to a dark horse, Rutherford B. Hayes, who had stood sixth on the first ballot of their convention. After graduating from Kenyon College, Hayes had studied law at Harvard and practiced in Ohio. Having answered the call to arms during the Civil War and risen to the office of Major General, he possessed the required military standing. Besides, he had been sent to the House of Representatives in Washington, and three times elected governor of Ohio. If not forceful, he had at least the weight of dignity. If not spectacular, he could with justice be called "a good man."

Whatever his qualifications, however, Hayes received a minority of the popular votes in the election of 1876, and perhaps a minority of the electoral votes. At any rate the outcome was disputed by the Democrats, and victory claimed for their candidate, Samuel J. Tilden. On the truth of the matter historians differ; but an electoral commission, on which Republicans had a majority, awarded the palm to Hayes. Coming into office under a cloud as had John Quincy Adams, and confronted by a Democratic House of Representatives throughout his term, and a Democratic Senate during the last two years, President Hayes could not strike out boldly, had he desired to do so. Hence nothing coming under the head of grand policy was associated with his administration. He withdrew the last of the federal troops from Southern capitals, fought the spoilsmen in his own party, and went out of office enjoying more public esteem than on the bitter day of his inauguration—a rare incident in American history.

JAMES A. GARFIELD

★★★

WITH the Democrats controlling both houses of Congress in 1880, Republicans were naturally disturbed by the outlook. One faction insisted that only a great military hero, General Grant, could be elected, and it put him at the top on the first ballot in the nominating convention. Another faction, fascinated by Blaine, put him second, while four other contenders trailed behind. For two days the convention pitched, tossed, and balloted until the deadlock was broken by a sudden landslide to a dark horse that had not appeared on the first ballot at all—James A. Garfield, from Ohio, the Valley of Democracy, where the memory of Andrew Jackson was still alive and had to be taken into account.

Although Garfield did not rank with Blaine in party affections, he had merits as a candidate. On the one side it could be pointed out that he was of humble origin and had worked as a boy on a canal boat; and on the other that he was a graduate of Williams College and had taught Greek and Latin in his youth. He likewise had a record of public service—in the state senate, in the Union Army as Major General, and in the House of Representatives. He was eloquent on the stump, hardworking, ingenious in negotiation, and had come through the scandals of the Grant administration politically secure, despite charges of corruption hurled against him by his foes. In any event he polled more votes than General Winfield S. Hancock, a military hero whom the Democrats cleverly put up against him. But this triumph President Garfield did not live long to enjoy, for four months after his inauguration in March he was shot down by a disappointed office seeker and, after a lingering illness, died in September.

CHESTER A. ARTHUR

THE Vice President, Chester A. Arthur, who assumed the presidency on the death of Garfield, in September, 1881, proved to be one of the great surprises of political history. To him the second place had fallen in 1880 as a result of a back-stage arrangement in the Republican convention. The Grant faction, headed by Roscoe Conkling of New York, baffled in its effort to nominate General Grant for a third term, insisted on some balm in the hour of defeat, and was allowed to pick the nominee for Vice President. To the dismay of the other party to the bargain, Conkling selected Chester A. Arthur, whose distinguishing services to his party and country had been rendered as collector of the port of New York. In fact he had been a notorious dispenser of spoils in the style consecrated by Martin Van Buren and had actually been removed from office by President Hayes for alleged violations of standards none too high at best.

But those who feared an unseemly scramble for spoils were happily disappointed in President Arthur. He had, it is true, played the political game according to rules in force since the advent of Jacksonian Democracy, but he possessed merits of his own. As the son of a Vermont clergyman, he had known religious discipline in his youth. A graduate of Union College, he had, presumably, some acquaintance with the learning of the past. Shadowed by the tragedy that raised him to power, President Arthur sought to meet his obligations bravely. Under his administration Congress struck the first effective blow at the spoils system by passing in 1883 the Civil Service Reform Act, which is still the basic law of the federal civil service. Indeed, the quality of his governance was so unexpectedly high that his friends thought him entitled to vindication by election in his own right. But that was not to be.

GROVER CLEVELAND

★★★

W HEN the election of 1884 approached, the devoted followers of James G. Blaine were determined that he should have the honor which had so long eluded his grasp. Charges of corruption still flew thick and fast around his head, but no other leader in the party enjoyed such popularity. At last the nomination came to him, and the Democrats answered the challenge by selecting as their candidate Grover Cleveland of New York. In Cleveland they found their worthy man. In origin he was humble enough; although, as the son of a Presbyterian clergyman in New Jersey, he could not boast of a log cabin background. But he had been left fatherless at the age of sixteen and had advanced in the world by hard work and self-denial—virtues warmly cherished by the American people. He had clerked in a store, taught school, kept books, and educated himself for the law. During the Civil War, while the Union Army was overcoming the Confederacy, Cleveland, as a lawyer in Buffalo, had given attention to his clients' affairs with a high degree of success. Locally noted for his diligence and party regularity, he had been elected sheriff of Erie county and then mayor of Buffalo. Thence his reputation for plain honesty spread and in 1882 he had been chosen governor of the state. A man who could carry New York, the Democrats assumed, might carry the country; and he did, by a narrow margin of a few hundred votes, after a campaign of vilification beyond brief description—indeed, any description.

President Cleveland found himself face to face with a Republican majority in the Senate, though supported by a Democratic House of Representatives. If he had formulated a legislative policy, he could hardly have brought it into effect. The one measure of special significance which he signed—the Interstate Commerce Act of 1887—could scarcely be ascribed in origin or form to him or the party which he headed. As executive, Cleveland vetoed pension bills by the score, fought "treasury grabs"—river and harbor bills pouring money into local "improvements"—and tried to prevent frauds in the distribution of the arable, mineral, and timber lands belonging to the Federal Government. In the course of this procedure he won for himself a reputation for possessing courage and honesty which, it seems, could not be assumed in public officials of that period.

In an unguarded moment, apparently, President Cleveland made an attack on the protective tariff in 1887 so slashing in manner that it could not be explained away later, when the Republicans made it an issue. In the campaign which ensued, he was defeated by Benjamin Harrison and temporarily retired to private life. Nominated again, for the third time in 1892, and elected, Cleveland set out on his second term with a Democratic Congress to aid him. But these four years were not to be as happy as the first. Protectionist Democrats joined Republicans in mangling the tariff bill on which the President's heart was set. Members of the new Populist party, speaking for discontented farmers, and radical Democrats inserted an income-tax clause into the measure—the second such provision in American history; and so Cleveland allowed it to become a law without his signature. Meanwhile the country was in the throes of the panic which broke in 1893. Mortgages by the thousand were foreclosed on farms; railways went into bankruptcy; poverty spread its hideous features over the land; strikes and labor disputes shocked "all friends of law and order." Populists threatened the gold standard by insisting that the Treasury should freely coin silver into money and make sixteen ounces of silver worth one of gold. Revolution broke out in Cuba, and Hawaii was filled with turmoil stirred up by American interests.

President Cleveland's dilemmas were many and great, but his actions were firm. On the advice of Richard Olney, his Secretary of State, a lawyer affiliated with railway interests, Cleveland sent federal troops to Chicago during the Pullman strike, against the protests of the Democratic governor of Illinois, John P. Altgeld. The strike leader, Eugene V. Debs, was sent to prison for violating an injunction issued by a federal court against strikers, and Altgeld was bluntly told to mind his own business. With equal resolution, Cleveland set his face against intervention in Cuba, the annexation of Hawaii, and all the imperialist ventures then on the horizon. With the same resolution he defended the gold standard against the Populists and silver advocates in his own party. He was assailed on the right and the left. His popularity steadily diminished. For a brief moment he diverted the divided nation by threatening Great Britain with war over a boundary question in Venezuela and by waving the Monroe Doctrine vigorously in the face of the Old World. But Great Britain yielded and no war came. In 1897 Grover Cleveland passed out of office rejected by his own party and disliked by the new imperialist school of Mahan, Lodge, Theodore Roosevelt, and John Hay.

BENJAMIN HARRISON

★★★

IN THE interval between Cleveland's first and second administrations, the White House was occupied by Benjamin Harrison, of Indiana. He too was a dark-horse candidate, for his name had been a low fifth on the first ballot in the Republican convention. Though short, stout, cold in manner, and rich, as riches went in Indianapolis, Harrison had some elements of popular appeal. He had worked in his youth on his father's farm in Ohio; he had served in the Civil War as a general; and he had been elected to the Senate of the United States by the Indiana legislature. He also had the advantage of coming from the Middle West, from a strategic state far removed from the taint of Wall Street, the symbol of the banking and industrial interests. All these things stood him in good stead. Then, of course, he had a crowning glory: he was a grandson of William Henry Harrison whom the Whigs had rushed to victory in the whirlwind, log cabin battle of 1840.

Besides having a candidate with personal qualifications, the Republicans derived benefits from an exciting event during the campaign. A clever person signing himself Charles F. Murchison wrote a letter to Lord Sackville, the British minister in Washington, asking him how to vote in the coming election.

The unwary Lord, in making his reply, hinted that the victory of the Democratic candidate would be more acceptable to England. This letter, given to the public late in the autumn, was seized upon by the Republicans, and the land was shaken by a roar against Great Britain that must have made the Hero of New Orleans turn over in his Tennessee grave. When the votes were counted it was found that Harrison had a majority of the electors, although the popular plurality was against him.

Taking advantage of the occasion, the Republican Congress drove through in 1890 the McKinley tariff bill raising protective duties to their highest point up to that time. But the promised prosperity did not immediately materialize and in the autumn of that year the Democrats captured the House of Representatives. Despite the fact that the Republicans made a grand gesture against monopoly by enacting the Sherman antitrust law, along with the McKinley tariff, they could not convince the country that they ought to be kept in power. When they renominated Harrison in 1892 and pitted him against Cleveland, the popular verdict was the most emphatic negative that the party had received in many a year. Something serious had happened; yet, as the election of 1896 demonstrated, nothing of a permanent nature.

WILLIAM McKINLEY

★★

B ETWEEN the great sectional conflict of 1860 and the
end of the century no political campaign rivaled in bit-
terness the struggle of 1896 which ended with the triumph of
William McKinley. Observing that the free silver advocates
and Populists were riding high in the Democratic party, the
Republicans came out against the free coinage of silver, except by international agreement, and declared in favor of a
firm foreign policy, intervention in Cuban affairs, a bigger
navy, and a high protective tariff. In reply to this defiance, the
Democrats went beyond Republican anticipations. They stole
the thunder of the Populists, who had built up a powerful third
party. They endorsed the free coinage of silver at the ratio of
sixteen to one, denounced the tariff as the mother of monopo-
lies, and assailed the Supreme Court for declaring void the
income tax law of 1894; they condemned federal interference
with local authorities in labor disputes, branding the issue of
labor-restraining injunctions by federal courts as a highly dangerous form of oppression. Thus issues were joined squarely
for the first time since 1860. To the Republicans the campaign
was a holy crusade of talents, respectability, and honor against
populism, socialism, communism, anarchy, and dishonor, then

regarded by most educated persons as one and the same thing. To the Democrats headed by William Jennings Bryan, it was an equally holy crusade of farmers, laborers, and humble people for security—for their homes and bread—against an embattled and corrupt plutocracy.

In their nominee the Republicans were peculiarly fortunate. William McKinley had sprung from humble and hardworking people (such as Bryan was now praising), and had climbed up the social ladder by diligence and self-sacrifice. Apart from a brief period at Allegheny College, his knowledge of the higher learning had been acquired by undirected studies. He served valiantly in the Union Army and emerged from the conflict a major in rank. Turning to law, he practiced successfully at Canton, Ohio, and after a few years' experience in local politics won a seat in the House of Representatives. There he distinguished himself as an advocate of high tariff protection, and gained the approval of those whose approval was important. From the House he went to the governor's office at Columbus in 1891, and was elected to the same post again in 1893.

Among McKinley's many friends was a businessman in Cleveland, Marcus A. Hanna, who, having acquired wealth, desired to play the role of Warwick, the king maker. It was, in no small measure, to the quiet leadership of Hanna and his ability to raise money for political uses, that McKinley owed his nomination and election. There had been managers before, in the days of Martin Van Buren and Thurlow Weed (who looked after Lincoln's interests in New York); but Hanna was unique in astuteness and in his power to command the confidence of great riches, while garnering in popular votes.

Victorious in a hard-fought campaign, the Republicans, under President McKinley's guidance, raised the tariff in 1897, postponing the firm establishment of the gold standard for three years, in fear of a battle with opposition Senators of the silver school. Having settled for the time the domestic issue of protection, they turned to strong foreign policy; waged war on Spain; freed Cuba and made it a protectorate; annexed Puerto Rico, Guam, and the Philippines; annexed Hawaii; joined other governments in suppressing the Boxer rebellion in China; and entered into the competition of European powers for prestige, commerce, and empire. America, said one of the orators, Albert Jeremiah Beveridge, had more manufactures and farm produce than could be used at home, and must seek outlets abroad in the traditional style set by Great Britain. In the election in 1900, voters were told that America had come of age, grown up, and must assume responsibilities for carrying Christianity, prosperity, liberty, and civilization to them that sat in darkness; and the voters enthusiastically replied by returning McKinley to office for another term. He had just taken up his second mandate when he was assassinated by an anarchist in the autumn of 1901, while opening an exposition at Buffalo, the third of the people's choices to fall a victim to violence.

Theodore Roosevelt

THEODORE ROOSEVELT

★★★

O N McKINLEY'S death executive authority passed to the
Vice President, Theodore Roosevelt, the first Republican President from the East. This young man, then in his forty-
third year, was a versatile personality—a well-born urbanite,
a sportsman, and a writer who felt competent to discourse on
many things. He had graduated from Harvard, travelled
abroad, served three years in the New York legislature, and
roughed it on a western ranch; he had been police commissioner in New York City, the place of his birth, a member of
the federal civil service commission, and Assistant Secretary of
the Navy. Besides, he had studied history and written many
volumes that had a popular appeal. Roosevelt, always eager
for adventure, welcomed the Spanish War, raised a regiment
of Rough Riders, and went over to the fray in Cuba. On his
return, the boss of New York, Thomas Platt, was looking for
a winner in the coming campaign for governor. Though Platt
disliked the young Colonel, he picked Roosevelt as the Republican candidate; and the voters of the state set their approval on the choice. Partly, if not entirely, for the purpose
of sidetracking the impetuous youth, Republicans forced
Roosevelt into the Vice President's office in 1900, and seasoned

statesmen among them were alarmed when the chief magistracy fell into his hands.

At the outset, however, President Roosevelt reassured them by promising to hold to the old course, and by retaining members of McKinley's cabinet. But in time, especially after his election in his own right in 1904, Roosevelt struck out for himself. He took advantage of nearly every occasion at home and abroad to announce his "policies." He advocated conservation of the forests, irrigation of waste lands, the dissolution of "bad" trusts, the imposition of income and inheritance taxes, and the stricter regulation of railways. He denounced "malefactors of great wealth" and militant labor leaders. He trafficked with Great Britain and Germany, sent agents to the conference of powers at Algeciras, dispatched a fleet around the world, helped to settle the Russo-Japanese war, made a secret agreement with Japan, entered into a gentlemen's understanding with Tokyo on the immigration question, and appointed delegates to the second Hague "peace" conference. He preached righteousness, denounced "mollycoddles," scolded conservative members of Congress, and supplied headlines for the newspapers almost every day. Near the close of his elective term, President Roosevelt selected his good friend, William H. Taft, the Secretary of War, as the best nominee for the Republicans, endorsed him in the campaign, turned over the presidency to the victor on March 4, 1909. Then Roosevelt went off to hunt lions in Africa, to visit courts in Europe, and to deliver lectures in France and England on "grand policy." Unconquerable in spirit, he could not retire to quiet life like Cleveland or Hayes, but was active in politics until overcome in 1919 by his last sleep. If some enduring achievements must be associated with his name, they may well be his contribution to the conservation of natural resources and the construction of the Panama Canal.

WILLIAM H. TAFT

★★★

A MERICANS who loved ease of mind doubtless heaved a
sigh of relief when William H. Taft supplanted the rest-
less Theodore Roosevelt in 1909. Everything about President
Taft suggested propriety, regularity, and tranquillity. He was
not a rough-rider, nor a rail-splitter, nor a planter. He was
born to urban wealth. His father had been a member of Grant's
cabinet, and a minister to Russia under Arthur. He himself
had been correctly educated at Yale, and had taken up the
practice of law at Cincinnati in the due course of time. At the
age of thirty-three young Taft entered public office and rose
from post to post—United States circuit judge, president of
the Philippine Commission, civil governor of the Philippines,
Secretary of War, secret emissary to Japan, to mention the
more important assignments. He was heavy in body, slow in
movement, genial in temper, conservative in thought—President Taft presented an almost complete antithesis to his predecessor, the apostle of the strenuous life who had chosen him
to lead the Republican party.

But despite Taft's love of peace every year of his administration was full of troubles. They began when he called a special
session of Congress in 1909 to revise the tariff—a thorny sub-

ject which Roosevelt had conveniently neglected. At the end he accepted a tariff bill so highly protectionist that Representatives and Senators of his own party were driven to vote against it. This split in his party he widened by trying to arrange a reciprocity tariff with Canada—another project deemed favorable to manufacturing interests in the United States. Western progressives he offended by assailing such newfangled notions as the initiative and referendum, which gave people the right to make laws by popular vote. Opponents of imperialism he alarmed by throwing the State Department into the promotion of foreign trade, under the frank slogan of "dollar diplomacy." Critics raised up by such policies and methods could not be placated by two bills competing with private enterprise, the postal savings bill and the parcel post bill, and by the proposal of two amendments to the Constitution—the one authorizing a federal income tax and the other popular election of United States Senators. President Taft had accepted these measures but it could not be said that they owed their existence to his imagination and resolve. Despite Taft's conciliatory efforts, Theodore Roosevelt entered the lists against him, tore a huge wing of progressives away from the Republican party, and helped to prevent his re-election in the campaign of 1912. Taft retired with great dignity to private life, refusing to employ his prestige to enrich himself by the practice of law. Yet he was not resigned enough to devote himself to meditation and the muses. He spent his time teaching at Yale and lecturing until called to the post of Chief Justice of the Supreme Court by President Harding.

Woodrow Wilson

WOODROW WILSON

★★

U NDERNEATH the pomp and circumstance of politics, accompanied by the endless struggle over the spoils of power, ran currents of ideas and interests which occasionally broke through the surface of things. In 1912 came such an upsurge. Although the outbreak had been prepared by the Populist movement, with its socialistic fringes, the origins of the distemper extended far back in American tradition to the days of Jefferson. For years, events and personalities had been preparing the way for another upheaval. Bryan had spread Populist ideas (See p. 95) throughout the Democratic party. Theodore Roosevelt had acquainted the Republicans with some of their features. Muckrakers, by unearthing scandals, had stirred suspicions about the perfection of American society. In their quest for a share of good things, women had demanded equal rights and privileges, including the suffrage. The growth of giant combinations in industry and trade unions among industrial workers had added to doubts and discontents. When President Taft failed to keep up the fight on "malefactors of great wealth," Theodore Roosevelt leaped into the arena again; and, when he failed to win the Republican nomination for himself, he split the party, taking off the progressive wing under his leadership in a struggle for the presidency.

Of the break in Republican ranks, long in process, the Democrats were excited observers. Taking advantage of the occasion, they put forward as their candidate Woodrow Wilson, then governor of New Jersey. The range of his appeal was wide. A son of a Virginia clergyman, who had practiced law at Atlanta, he offered a pleasing aspect to the South. As professor and president at Princeton, he had long been known as a conservative, in fact, as a disciple of Edmund Burke. He had been opposed to free silver, to popular election of Senators, to woman's suffrage, and to all such "heresies." He had wanted to see Bryan, one of his competitors for the candidacy, "knocked into a cocked hat." Wilson was acceptable to the conservative East, despite taints of low-tariff doctrines. In his later years, however, he had acquired a reputation for "progressivism." He had approved the initiative and referendum (See p. 110), workmen's compensation, and the regulation of public utilities—so popular in the West.

In the campaign of 1912 Wilson defined the issue as a conflict between consolidated wealth, which, he alleged, had long dominated the Government at Washington, and the small man eager for a chance to get into business for himself—the small man to be found everywhere in the United States. Under the slogan of "the new freedom," he proposed to restore the blessings of *laissez faire*, or free competition of individuals without government interference. Elected by a minority of the voters, owing to the split in the opposition, President Wilson displayed a will of his own. He drove the Democratic Congress to its tasks. The tariff was lowered. A more drastic law designed to dissolve the trusts was enacted. The banking system was overhauled, with a gesture to states' rights in the form of twelve federal reserve bank districts. Small farmers received their portion in the shape of federal land banks empowered to lend them money at lower rates of interest. To organized labor two morsels were handed. One purported to limit the use of injunctions in labor disputes—a provision soon riddled by the courts. The other forced railways to grant an eight hour day for trainmen.

When his domestic program was completed, Wilson turned more earnestly than ever to the problem of the great war then raging in Europe. He feared the triumph of Germany as a threat to the security of the United States, even in the Western Hemisphere, though he was formally neutral. In upholding the rights of American nationals to sell goods and lend money to the Entente powers, he made commitments and created interests all pointing in the direction of American participation in the war. Re-elected by a narrow margin in 1916, when his campaign managers emphasized the fact that he had "kept us out of the war," and made a special bid for the votes of women in California, President Wilson led the country into World War I in the spring of 1917.

In their desperation, the Allies accepted his idea of the conflict in Europe as a war for democracy to end war. Gaining their full pound of flesh and more in the Versailles treaty of peace, they also allowed President Wilson to include the Covenant of the League of Nations in the body of the treaty itself. Then Wilson faced a crisis at home. The Republicans, victorious in the congressional elections of 1918, turned furiously against him and his League. After weeks of wrangling they prevented the ratification of the treaty by the Senate and sent his high hopes crashing to earth. America was to be "isolated," not a member of the League of Nations.

WARREN G. HARDING

★★★

I F THE election of 1920 was a verdict on the War and the
League of Nations, it was decisive; for the Republicans,
marshalled behind Warren G. Harding, overwhelmed James
Cox, the Democratic candidate, in a landslide at the polls. It
was a mass victory, not a personal triumph for the victor.
It meant, Harding said, a return to normalcy, which in turn
meant a restoration of the principles and practices associated
with his idols, William McKinley and Marcus A. Hanna, pro-
fessors and practitioners in the Ohio school of politics. The
new President said nothing contrary to that tradition either
before or during the campaign. He himself belonged to it and
was among the loyal residents of "Main Street."

After a meager education at local schools and the Central
College, Harding had entered the newspaper business at
Marion, Ohio, not far from his birthplace. At the age of thirty-
five he began a public career as a member of the state legislature. Then he stepped upward to the office of lieutenant governor. Though defeated as a candidate for governor, he later
managed to find his way into the United States Senate, where
he became noted for conviviality, not for anything positive in
the way of program. He was in fact a hail fellow well met, a

good poker player, and a gay companion. Yet on occasion he could display an impressive dignity, and speak with sonorous gravity.

Under President Harding's general superintendence, the tariff was raised to new heights, as if with a gesture to the McKinley heritage. The weight of the Departments of Commerce, State, and Navy was thrown vigorously behind "the policy of national interest," known under President Taft as "dollar diplomacy." Strikers on railways were pursued by sweeping injunctions; and William H. Taft was made Chief Justice of the Supreme Court. But at the same time a decided effort was made to check the naval competition which the United States had entered in the closing years of the nineteenth century. At a conference of the great powers held in Washington, in 1921-22, the Secretary of State, Charles E. Hughes, cut the knot by proposing a naval holiday in battleship construction, and arrived at a temporary ratio with Great Britain and Japan which stabilized the construction of capital ships. Making a humane gesture to the left, President Harding released from prison Eugene V. Debs, the outstanding Socialist, who had been convicted during Wilson's administration for opposing the war.

Had untoward circumstances not intervened, President Harding might have enjoyed a course of normalcy. Unfortunately for him, however, he had brought to Washington, along with the "best minds" in the party, some companions on pelf and pleasure bent. Opportunities for peculation were multitudinous—in winding up the affairs of the custodian of alien property worth millions, in the sale of the Government's merchant ships, in the enforcement of prohibition established in 1921, in the enormous outlays for the care of war veterans, and in the administration of rich oil lands transferred from the Navy Department to the Department of the Interior, where presided Albert B. Fall.

Before many months had passed, scandals broke. The head of the veterans' bureau was forced to resign; later he was indicted and sent to the penitentiary. Other difficulties, even more serious, were brewing when President Harding died suddenly in the summer of 1923. Speaking years afterward at the dedication of a Memorial, President Hoover said the best that could be said when he remarked that President Harding had been "betrayed by a few men whom he had trusted, by men who, he had believed, were his devoted friends." But whether the irregularities of his administration were greater than those under previous or subsequent administrations, historical inquiry has not yet disclosed.

CALVIN COOLIDGE

★★★

THE obligations which President Harding relinquished fell to the Vice President, Calvin Coolidge, son of a Vermont farmer and storekeeper. In the arts of American politics none was more skilled than he; few more blessed by accidents in line with his own fortunes. Young Coolidge had been elected a member of the city council four years after his graduation at Amherst College in 1895, while he was practicing law in Northampton, Massachusetts. Henceforward he was almost continually in office, rising higher and higher—city solicitor, clerk of the courts, member of the lower house of the state legislature, mayor, state senator, lieutenant governor, and governor. Prudent, frugal, and with a reputation for the silence which is golden, Calvin Coolidge entered upon his presidential heritage, and conducted public affairs with such circumspection that he was elected in his own right in 1924.

In the course of President Coolidge's administration, some of the chief malefactors belonging to the Harding régime were prosecuted and sent to prison, oil lands fraudulently seized were recovered, the Attorney General, Harry M. Daugherty, was forced out of office, and numerous scandals cleared up with resolution and discretion. Meanwhile the income tax was reduced, especially in the higher brackets; a subsidy was voted to shipping, in the form of lucrative mail contracts; assistance was given to the infant aviation industry; and the weight of government was lent to the promotion of foreign commerce. With the country prosperous, according to prevailing standards of prosperity, President Coolidge might well have commanded a second elective term; but he did not choose it and it was not forced upon him by the Republican convention of 1928. So he passed into retirement amid a blaze of success. For many months the memory of happy days under his presidency was to linger in the minds of beneficiaries; but efforts to "recover" them could not disclose his secret.

HERBERT C. HOOVER

★★★

DURING the campaign which carried him into office Herbert C. Hoover expressed the opinion that a continuation of Republican policies would banish any poverty remaining in the United States. Agriculture, no doubt, had long been in distress, there was some unemployment, and misery appeared in certain spots; but the prospects for "making everybody rich" seemed by no means wholly utopian. And the American electorate evidently thought that Mr. Hoover possessed the qualifications for the promising task ahead. He was of the American democratic tradition. The son of an Iowa blacksmith, reared on a farm, educated in public schools, and graduated from Stanford University, he belonged to the powerful school of politics which exalts rising in the world.

Besides, he had enjoyed unique business experience. He had embarked upon engineering as a career, and spent the better part of twenty years as a mining prospector, promoter, and reorganizer in Asia, Australia, Africa, and Europe, accumulating an independent fortune in the process. Mr. Hoover sprang into international prominence, from his station in London at the outbreak of World War I, as the administrator of Belgian relief funds, and after the United States entered the conflict he served the Government in various capacities. So great was his distinction in 1920 that Republicans and Democrats alike looked to him as a prospective leader. Although uncertain for a moment, he finally cast in his lot with the Republicans; and under President Harding he entered the cabinet as Secretary of Commerce—a post which he continued to hold until his nomination for President.

Secretary Hoover, while engaged in promoting domestic and foreign trade, made many contacts with business directors and built up a following and a reputation for sagacity that served him well in 1928. In a whirlwind he overcame his opponent, Alfred E. Smith, and took office on March 4, 1929, under auspicious skies. With a view to relieving the distresses of farmers, President Hoover called a special session of Congress and sponsored an agricultural marketing act with price maintenance features, which cost the Treasury at least $500,-000,000. He accepted from the same Congress, as if in remembrance of William McKinley, a new tariff bill making rates still higher, though apparently dubious about the wisdom of the measure.

But while the tariff measure was on the carpet, the great business boom exploded, with a resounding crash on the New York stock market, in the autumn of 1929. America in common with other industrial countries, then entered upon the most devastating economic crisis in the long history of such maladies. Trying to keep the ship as steady as possible President Hoover urged business leaders not to be frightened and to hold up buying power by the payment of good wages. He planned an enlargement of federal public works to provide employment, and called upon state and local authorities to follow this example. He proposed and obtained the creation of the Reconstruction Finance Corporation, empowered to lend money to banks, railways, states, municipalities, and other agencies in need of cash. He insisted, however, that immediate poor relief for the unemployed, in accordance with American custom, belonged to private charity and local communities. Still the crisis deepened and widened. The inevitable opposition grew. In the election of 1930 the Democrats captured the House of Representatives, if by a narrow margin. No President, except Monroe in 1820, had ever survived a major economic crisis, and so the customary fate befell President Hoover in his quest for re-election and vindication in 1932, namely, retirement to private life. Yet after a season of silence, he began to dispatch messages to the nation from his home in Palo Alto on liberty and the mission of the Republican party.

FRANKLIN D. ROOSEVELT

★★

FORESEEING a Democratic year, Franklin D. Roosevelt entered the presidential contest from his strategic post of Governor of New York. He had many qualifications. He was an Eastern man, a graduate of Harvard, who had acquired political practice as member of the state legislature, Assistant Secretary of the Navy under President Wilson, and candidate for Vice President in 1920. Stricken by illness and coming out of it with paralyzed legs, he nevertheless rallied to the support of Alfred E. Smith's candidacy for President in 1928, and won the office of governor for himself. Re-elected in 1930, Mr. Roosevelt demonstrated that he "knew the ropes" and could collect votes. As the Democratic candidate for President in 1932, he conducted the campaign on the well-known practice that avoidance of mistakes was the supreme necessity. So few, if any, concrete issues were joined in the contest, but one telling figure was introduced to the public: "the forgotten man" who was promised "a new deal."

On the day of President Roosevelt's inauguration the depression had taken on the signs of national distress and alarm. Banks were closed in all parts of the country. Unemployment was mounting. Poverty was spreading. With a speed and firmness which surprised those who imagined the President to be "an amiable dilettante," he embarked upon a remarkable program of administration and legislation. By executive order under an old statute, he shut all banks and arranged to reopen only those that were "sound"—the great majority, as time proved. The gold standard was abandoned and a managed currency, with a flexible unit, substituted. Having grappled with the immediate emergency, he then launched his recovery drive.

The powers of the Reconstruction Finance Corporation were enlarged to include making loans to nearly everyone in distress who could offer some security. Land banks were reorganized, farm loans converted, interest rates reduced, and credit facilities extended in agriculture. The age-long trust question was attacked openly by the National Industrial Recovery Act. It allowed the industries to form associations and draw up codes under federal supervision, coupled with a promise of collective bargaining to organized labor. But it was declared unconstitutional in its main features by the Supreme Court in May, 1935. Arrangements were made by the Agricultural Adjustment Act for the organization of agriculture, the curtailment of special crops to the limits of "effective demand," and the channeling of money, raised by taxation, into the pockets of farmers in return for their pledges to reduce the output.

To the integration of industry and agriculture was added a program for "social security" submitted by President Roosevelt and adopted by Congress in 1935. These measures included federal assistance to states in establishing old-age pensions and unemployment insurance. Meanwhile, to afford immediate relief, the federal government allocated billions of dollars to provide food, clothing, and shelter for an army of sufferers, which was placed at 22,000,000 in the fifth year of the depression. More billions were voted in 1935—with a view to diminishing direct relief and providing employment—for housing projects, rural rehabilitation, rural electrification, grade-crossing removal, the conservation of natural resources, public works, and other projects that would not compete with private business. Never before in American history had the forgotten man, and many others, been remembered so lavishly, as the national debt bequeathed by World War I mounted higher and higher.

Among the measures passed by Congress at its 1935 session was a series of laws touching nearly every phase of domestic and foreign affairs. Aids to agriculture were continued and extended. The right of labor to organize freely and bargain collectively with employers was reasserted in the National Labor Relations Act. Pensions for railway employees were authorized. Electrical utilities engaged in interstate transmission of power were brought under federal supervision; and the dissolution of great holding companies of wide range was ordered. The banking business was taken more closely under national control. Special taxes were laid on large incomes and the estates of "the very rich."

Still in the sixth year of the depression, the jam did not break. Great railway companies were in bankruptcy and others on the verge of calamity. American industry hobbled along, turning out forty or fifty billion dollars' worth of goods, although its equipment could have supplied about three times that amount. Only war was to put it back into full employment, war of which forebodings appeared. While the country was better off in 1936 than it had been in 1932 great distress still afflicted it.

Nominated by the Democratic convention for a second term in 1936, the President won an overwhelming victory in the election. His second term was marked by new measures in the interest of "one third of a nation, ill-housed, ill-clad, ill-nourished," as he described it. Feeling that the Supreme Court was blocking his measures of reform, President Roosevelt called on Congress to allow him the right to appoint new justices, up to the number of six, in case justices reaching the age of seventy did not resign. Thus the Court might have been increased from nine to sixteen. But Congress sharply refused to adopt his plan.

In the course of President Roosevelt's second term wars broke out in Asia and Europe. Japan began war on China in 1937. The German dictator, Adolf Hitler, attacked Poland in September, 1939; and Great Britain and France replied by declaring war on Germany. The next year, the Italian dictator, Benito Mussolini, joined Germany in the great war in Europe.

With Europe and Asia ablaze, President Roosevelt gave special attention to foreign affairs. On October 5, 1937, in a speech at Chicago, he proposed that the peace-loving nations should join in applying a "quarantine" to the aggressors. Early the following year he asked Congress to authorize a great increase in the Navy. After war began in Europe, in September, 1939, he induced Congress to modify the Neutrality Act and permit the sale of munitions to foreign countries—in effect, to Great Britain and the other powers at war with Germany, Italy, and Japan.

Amid these circumstances, the Democratic convention in 1940 nominated President Roosevelt for a third term. Thus it broke the third-term tradition followed since the days of George Washington. In his campaign President Roosevelt advocated giving aid to the countries at war with Germany, Italy, and Japan. At the same time he assured the American people that "this country is not going to war." In the election, President Roosevelt was easily victorious over the Republican candidate, Wendell Willkie.

After his victory, the President concentrated on foreign affairs and war measures. On his recommendation Congress passed, in March, 1941, the Lend-Lease Bill, which empowered the President to supply munitions and other goods in immense amounts to Great Britain and the other powers at war with Germany, Italy, and Japan. On May 27, 1941, President Roosevelt proclaimed a state of unlimited national emergency. In August he and Winston Churchill, the British Prime Minister, held a conference "somewhere" in the Atlantic, agreed on steps to be taken against the aggressors, and issued a statement, called the Atlantic Charter, which set forth lofty promises of a better world after the war.

Meanwhile relations between the United States and Japan approached a breaking point. Finally, November 26, 1941, the Secretary of State, Cordell Hull, gave the American terms in plain language to the Japanese government. Without any warning, on December 7, 1941, Japanese armed forces attacked the American stronghold in the Hawaiian Islands, and then plunged southward in the Pacific. Soon Germany and Italy declared war on the United States and the world was aflame.

Besides serving as Commander in Chief of American armed forces in combat around the globe, President Roosevelt took personal charge of foreign affairs, and became the country's most widely travelled President. At a meeting with Prime Minister Churchill in Casablanca, January, 1943, he proclaimed "unconditional surrender" as the supreme war aim of the powers arrayed against Germany, Italy, Japan, and their "satellites." This doctrine was also accepted by Russia, which had been in the war since Hitler's attack on Russia in June, 1941. Later in the year 1943 the President met with Churchill and General Chiang Kai-shek at Cairo; and still later, with Churchill and Joseph Stalin, head of the Russian government, at Teheran. Two years later, in 1945, after his election for a fourth term in 1944, he conferred with Churchill and Stalin at Yalta on war measures and war aims. In the meantime, he labored on the project for a new world organization to be established by the victorious nations—a project which bore fruit in the United Nations Charter drafted at San Francisco.

With victory in the war at last fully in sight, President Roosevelt, worn out by his labors, died suddenly on April 12, 1945, at Warm Springs, Georgia, where he had long been wont to seek rest and relief from the burdens of his great office.

HARRY S. TRUMAN

★★★

THE sudden death of Franklin D. Roosevelt on April 12, 1945, hurled Vice President Harry S. Truman into the highest office in the land. By contrast with his popular and seasoned predecessor, who had held the helm as Chief Executive for the record-breaking period of over twelve years, Mr. Truman was relatively unknown and certainly untried at the labors of global management. Though he was modestly worried about how the nation would take this drastic change in leadership, the transition went off smoothly.

There was nothing in his early life to indicate he might rise so high. Born in a small Missouri town, raised on a farm, he tried many things. After doing minor clerical jobs, he went back to the family farm. Off to Europe in World War I, he tasted victory as an artillery captain, but on his return went down to civilian defeat, overwhelmed by debt in a small haberdashery venture. Rescued from this mishap by the powerful and corrupt Pendergast political machine in Kansas City and elected county judge, he began his political career. In 1934 he was elected United States Senator from Missouri and won re-election in 1940. As Chairman of a

Senate investigating committee on wastes in war and defense spending, he attracted wide attention by his industry and fairness, shortly before being nominated, as Roosevelt's choice, and elected Vice President on the Democratic ticket in 1944.

With this modest background, Mr. Truman faced a stupendous task at the international level as he took the oath of office. He had to conclude America's participation in the most extensive war it had fought and discuss peace settlements with friends and foes holding widely divergent views. He was confronted with occupation problems in Germany, Austria and Japan. These assignments were greatly complicated by his limited familiarity with Roosevelt's secret understandings with Churchill and Stalin.

At first, Truman was swept along by the momentum of things started under Roosevelt. Shortly after he took office, an international gathering at San Francisco began to draft the United Nations Charter. While it was at work, Germany collapsed on May 8, 1945. Just as he was about to discuss Germany's fate with the British and Russians at Potsdam, he received news that America at last had a successful atomic bomb. Promptly, he told Japan to give up or face "utter destruction." On August 6, 1945, a new era in warfare opened with the dropping by his orders of an atomic bomb, that laid waste to Hiroshima. Less than five months after he became President, Japan surrendered.

With the enemy powers out of the running, Mr. Truman now confronted an insatiable victor—Communist Russia. Experiencing trouble in dealing with the Communist menace through the United Nations, he declared on March 12, 1947, that the United States must, where necessary, bypass that body and act directly to block Communist expansion. In line with this so-called "Truman Doctrine" he secured power from Congress to extend American aid to Greece and Turkey, then shadowed by Communist aggression. At his behest, Congress broadened American economic and military assistance to encompass other countries resisting Russian pressure, from the chief powers of Western Europe to lesser nations such as Iran.

In Asia, the Communist drive carried very far. Through General Marshall, he undertook to get the Chinese Nationalist Government to make major concessions to the Chinese Communists in return for continued American aid. When the Communists substituted conquest for compromise and made a rapid sweep of the Chinese mainland, Mr. Truman could salvage little from the wreckage. After he pulled American troops from nearby South Korea, the Russian-backed North Koreans seized the occasion to invade their neighbor. It was at this late and critical juncture that Mr. Truman tried a swift reversal of policy; without asking Congress to declare war, he threw American troops into a United Nations action in Korea. When the North Koreans were reinforced by masses of Chinese Communists and a major conflict developed, there seemed to be no simple solution. He neither wished to withdraw on unfavorable terms nor risk lighting the fuse for World War III by attacking Chinese strength at its source.

On the home front, Mr. Truman was heir to the policies of President Roosevelt, for whom he had labored faithfully as a Senator. The programs he submitted to Congress for extending federal activities were more or less along familiar Rooseveltian New Deal lines, ranging from suggested increases in social security coverage and compulsory national health insurance to ventures in economic stabilization through wage and price controls. He retained numerous powers granted during World War II by postponing official recognition of the cessation of hostilities until well after the Japanese surrender. During labor disputes he was active, ordering the Government on occasion to seize and operate privately-owned railroads, soft coal mines and oil refineries.

Many Americans were reluctant to continue and enlarge the network of federal controls. The Japanese collapse produced an urge to scrap burdensome wartime restrictions. Aware of this, Congress refused a number of President Truman's requests for new or extended authority. After he had attacked the Democratic Congress for its stand, the nation elected an even more antagonistic Republican majority to that body in 1946. The sympathy with which the nation had first greeted him was being evaporated by the heat of politics. Undaunted by two years of struggle with the new Congress, Mr. Truman ran for President on the Democratic ticket in 1948. Now his troubles multiplied. Some Southern Democrats, abhorring his views on civil rights, bolted the Party to favor Mr. J. Strom Thurmond for President; other, more radical Democrats deserted to help Mr. Henry A. Wallace, the Progressive candidate optimistically seeking better relations with Russia. With hard-hitting tours totalling over 30,000 miles, punctuated by many "whistle-stop" speeches, Mr. Truman won a victory over the Republican candidate, Governor Thomas E. Dewey, upsetting predictions of some of the sagest poll-takers. The contest was so close, however, that Mr. Truman received less than half the popular vote in that year of split affections, becoming the first minority President since 1912.

In Truman's second term, the expenses of the Korean contest were mainly met by high taxes at the national level. For this and other reasons, during his service as President, the Federal Government collected more revenue from the American people than it had gathered under all the previous Presidents combined, over a span of more than a hundred and fifty years. Yet this enormous intake, offset in part by the diminished buying power of the dollar, did not balance the budget consistently. When Truman retired, the national debt was several billion dollars above the record set under his immediate predecessor.

With such enormous sums in circulation, it is not surprising that portions of it were carelessly handled. Charges of corruption were raised that included the squandering of funds in the purchase of supplies, the use of political influence for a fee to obtain attractive government loans and contracts, and tax adjustments for favored parties. In keeping with his notions of party loyalty, Mr. Truman proved somewhat slow to sweep his administration of deficient personnel. This reluctance, coupled with public alarm over Communist infiltration in Washington offices, had dissipated some of the enthusiasm of his followers by 1952, when the Democratic Party again went before the people to defend its record.

Under Democratic sway, a great war had been won, a high level of prosperity had been maintained in post-war years, and through the development of atomic weapons the armed might of America had been brought to an historic peak. At the same time, there was rising dissatisfaction with many aspects of the management of affairs at home, and with continued police action abroad. Not sharing his immediate predecessor's apparently unquenchable zeal for the Presidency, Mr. Truman now wearied of the fray, declining to try for another term in 1952. Returning to his Missouri homeland in 1953, he brought to an end the long era during which there had been no legal limits on the length of time one could remain in the office of President; under the Twenty-second Amendment to the Constitution, adopted in 1951, none of his successors can stay in power for over ten years.

Out of office, but remaining deeply interested in politics, Mr. Truman wrote his memoirs and emerged from the sidelines occasionally to take a hand in the work of his party, especially in presidential election years.

DWIGHT D. EISENHOWER

★★

FTER losing five presidential elections in monotonous
succession, the Republicans tried in 1952 a device that
had often helped save the day for hard-pressed parties in the
past—that of backing a famous soldier for the presidency. Their
candidate, General Dwight D. Eisenhower, had graduated
from West Point in 1915, embarked on a long army career
and risen rapidly to prominence after the 1941 attack on Pearl
Harbor. In 1943, he became supreme commander of the allied
forces organized for the invasion and conquest of Western
Europe. Success in that capacity brought him renown, and
subsequent high military assignments kept his name before the
public. He had the further advantage of having hitherto
avoided domestic politics, thus raising no annoying set of old
memories to plague his party on election day.

Times were favorable for such a venture. The nation was
still engaged in the costly Korean struggle which, it was feared,
might develop into global war. The General's promise, if he
won, to visit the scene of action before inauguration, was attractive to voters. Many hoped he could not only terminate that
local conflict but cope with Communist plans for expansion
elsewhere. Striving to overcome the momentum of his candi-

dacy, the Democrats were in the embarrassing position of having themselves once viewed him as a good man to put on their own ticket. By contrast the Democratic candidate, Adlai E. Stevenson, was comparatively obscure on the national stage. Stevenson's lot was further complicated by President Truman's energetic efforts on his behalf, entangling the candidate in the public mind with the by now none-too-popular Truman record. When the returns were in, it was found that the General had achieved a smashing victory.

ʲIt was indeed a gala celebration that the long-repressed Republicans staged when, for the first time in twenty years, they inaugurated a President on January 20, 1953. Their new leader brought satisfaction to the internationalist wing of the party by breaking with Republican isolationist traditions, and continuing instead the global patterns of thought of recent Democratic chief executives. Whereas he had previously been a mere instrument for carrying out Roosevelt's and Truman's orders for the management of American and associated forces in Europe in the struggle for power played with Russia, he was now in full command of American efforts in his own right and had, in Secretary of State Dulles, a seasoned diplomatic aide. Eisenhower embraced the Truman Doctrine that Russian-dominated Communism must be contained by strong international effort. He conferred with foreign chiefs in the grand manner of recent Democratic Presidents, holding top-level meetings, for example, at Geneva in 1955 with high British, French and Russian officials. Moreover, Eisenhower often described his foreign operations in terms of "justice" and "international morality" in a manner reminiscent of Democratic Presidents as far back as Woodrow Wilson.

On the other hand, Eisenhower displayed his own distinct judgment in the military field, avoiding getting caught in ill-conceived, far-away ventures. Familiar with Korean fighting from his pre-inauguration trip to the scene, he had cease-fire negotiations successfully concluded shortly after becoming President. Thenceforth, despite provocations and appeals for help, he steadfastly refrained from throwing American troops into actual combat anywhere.

Meanwhile, he strengthened mutual defense arrangements with a chain of countries ringing the Soviet Union and Red China, all the way from Western Europe to Japan. To friendly lands he sent military supplies. From bases abroad he even maintained, for a time, a watch by air on installations inside Russia.

Eisenhower followed Truman's practice of granting monetary and technical assistance to lands outside the Communist camp. At his behest, Congress voted billions for the purpose, as it had done under his Democratic predecessors. Eisenhower also made several good-will trips abroad, cancelling others because of hostile foreign demonstrations.

Under Eisenhower, too, strenuous efforts were made to meet, if not surpass, Russian missile successes by developing American missiles with atomic warheads, capable of hitting targets thousands of miles away in a matter of minutes. During his administration, numerous missiles were placed on land in a position to fire, and the first nuclear-powered missile-carrying American submarine went to sea. Elaborate steps were taken for defense, including the building and operation of complex air raid warning systems.

Eisenhower backed a prime strategic concept—mass retaliation against an enemy by means and at places of our own choosing. It envisioned deadly raids from scattered bases to destroy the enemy homeland with nuclear weapons. Yet Eisenhower dreaded the consequences. He frankly admitted that mass attack and mass retaliation might leave so little of either participant as to make the operation "unthinkable" in a civilized society. Did this spell the end of the era of global warfare, as many fondly hoped, or would American strategy be altered to permit some less severe but "more practical" type of fighting? Time holds the answer.

Very different were the problems of domestic politics. In a rare act of political chivalry, Truman invited Eisenhower and his administrative team to visit Washington and familiarize themselves with their impending jobs in advance of inauguration day (a courtesy that Eisenhower, in his turn, extended to his Democratic successor eight years later).

Following this unique transition, Eisenhower strove to get along easily with Congress by conferences, suggestions, and negotiations. No longer forced into line as they had been under some Democrats, members of Congress enjoyed the change in pace—too well, some commentators added. Eventually, Eisenhower, an excellent coordinator, evolved an easy-going "middle of the road" technique aimed at winning coalition support from fractions of both parties.

Appealing to liberal Democrats for help, he followed the New Deal line on certain matters. Thus he got Congress to extend social security coverage to several million more people, and obtained a revised farm aid program under which his administration distributed over five billion dollars to hard-hit agriculture in a single year.

On the other hand, his middle of the road program did offer conservative Republicans an administration that was more friendly toward business than its predecessor. He allowed existing laws setting federal controls over wages, prices and rents quietly to expire. He let labor and management settle a great steel strike in their own way. Representatives of big business entered his Cabinet. Heavy excess profits taxes imposed on corporations under Truman died, freeing more company funds for plant expansion and dividends. The gross national output of goods and services, measured in dollars, continued the vigorous climb started under Truman and reached new highs. The stock market took an upward leap.

This setting, coupled with a war scare in the Suez Canal region, rallied voters around his peace and prosperity banner in the presidential elections of 1956, enabling him to defeat Democrat Adlai E. Stevenson once more, by a larger margin than in 1952. When the dust of battle settled, however, it was seen that Eisenhower had outrun the rest of his party. Facing a Democratic majority in both houses of Congress throughout his second term, he tried no striking changes in policy. Yet he managed to finish off his administration with a considerable show of strength, by relying on the veto and the help of conservative Southern Democrats to hold the line against certain large Democratic spending projects.

During his eight years in the White House, he had preserved his popularity with a good record as a man in quest of peace with justice. The economy had been kept on a fairly even keel, and Communist plans had been thwarted at many points. Nevertheless some held he had not done enough; that Communist inroads were being made still, in Asia, Africa and Latin America and that he had remained too much on the sidelines during the tricky 1960 election period. His less than adroit handling of such incidents as the shooting down of the American U-2 spy plane in Russia further clouded his international record and his costly budgets, his approach to the farm problem, and his failure to revitalize the Republican party sufficiently, disappointed some of his supporters at home.

Summing up his philosophy on the verge of his departure from the White House, in a "middle of the road" farewell address to the American people, he called for a balance between the public and the private economy, and between actions helpful for the moment and the welfare of future generations. Then, he warned against the dangers inherent in an arms race. Recognizing the need for strong defenses, he pointed out that they also necessitate the existence of a great military-industrial complex and that "we must guard against the acquisition of unwarranted influence" by it. That is, while the "potential for the disastrous rise of misplaced power exists and will persist," he said, we "must never let the weight of this combination endanger our liberties or our democratic processes."

JOHN F. KENNEDY

★★★

O N INAUGURATION DAY, 1961, the oldest man
yet to serve as President, Dwight D. Eisenhower, 70
years of age, turned his office over to John F. Kennedy, at 43
not only the youngest man yet elected to that post, but at
the time, by far the youngest head of any major world power.

The prime driving force behind Kennedy's fast rise had
been a dynamic, closely-knit family of Catholics of Irish
extraction with a background of activity in Democratic politics. The head of the household, Joseph P. Kennedy, had
fought through anti-Catholic and anti-Irish discrimination to
become one of the nation's wealthiest men and American
Ambassador to Great Britain. After leaving the latter post,
he turned to promoting the political ventures of his sons. The
oldest of these to survive World War II was John F. Kennedy, who had served in the Navy with distinction under
fire. An honor graduate of Harvard University, well read,
he had the education and means for entering politics at a relatively high intellectual level. With widely ramified family
backing, he was elected from Massachusetts first to the lower
house of Congress, then to the Senate. Barely missing the
nomination for Vice-President in 1956, he went on to win the
Democratic candidacy for President in 1960. While he soon
outran his 47-year-old Republican opponent, Nixon, at the

polls, he accomplished it by the narrowest margin in over fifty years—less than two-tenths of one percent of the popular vote.

Kennedy's victory was due to a unique combination of forces. First of all, by his ability to challenge and outmaneuver older, more established politicians, he had become popular with many young voters. He had also rallied around him men and women of his own faith in the first successful effort to place a member of the Catholic minority in the White House. Through attacks on racial and religious bigotry, too, he had won the sympathy and support of other minority groups. Finally, he had managed to get the critical aid he needed from tolerant and influential majorities.

The new President opened his administration with an eloquent Inauguration Address affirming America's resolve to stand firmly by its friends abroad in the cause of freedom. Yet, less than three months later, that resolve was tested and found wanting. In April, 1961, as groups of Cuban refugees he had encouraged to invade their Communist-held homeland were being attacked at their Bay of Pigs landing site, he denied them American help. Attempting to recover prestige after this disastrous failure Kennedy, by a display of firmness, held West Berlin, Germany, in the face of Russian threats and moves. While he was doing this, however, the Russians were working feverishly in Cuba to complete a nuclear missile system capable of wrecking many major American cities in a matter of minutes. Caught in the act, if belatedly, by American reconnaisance, and finding their shipments of missiles cut off by a strong naval patrol, the Russians backed down. At Kennedy's insistence they pulled their missiles out of Cuba and dismantled bases but Cuba itself remained a center for Communist intrigue and sabotage.

Viewed in its entirety, Kennedy's record in the foreign field fell far short of the goals he set for himself in his Inaugural Address. True, Americans still held West Berlin but elsewhere—especially in Southeast Asia, Africa, and Latin America, important ground had been lost to Communism. Only in small measure had these reverses been offset by such prestige-building enterprises as the work of Peace Corps volunteers on overseas projects.

To take charge of his domestic concerns, Kennedy brought together the youngest set of cabinet officers in many years— one of them being his brother and close adviser, Attorney-General Robert F. Kennedy. The President also surrounded himself with a young "brain trust" drawn from academic circles. At times, this administration operated with boldness. For example, the President and his brother, the Attorney General, used large numbers of troops to defy mobs and enforce a court order calling for the registration of a Negro at the University of Mississippi. Kennedy also made headlines with a sharp attack on a steel executive for raising prices, but in the process lost so much of the confidence of businessmen that a precipitous drop on the stock market ensued. Most dramatic of all, was the Kennedy administration's decision to climax a long series of preparations begun under Eisenhower by lifting the first Americans into outer space, via capsules that orbited the globe, then to follow this with plans to land men on the moon.

On the other hand, Kennedy accomplished little on the legislative front. Having been elected by a very slim majority, he was unable to put much pressure on Congress. While he did get some of his proposals enacted, such as one calling for a rise in minimum wage rates, more often he was rebuffed, as was the case with his proposed cut in income taxes and his plan for broadening medical assistance to the aged.

As he was nearing the end of his difficult initial term in office, Kennedy was hoping to strengthen his position with a major victory in the elections of 1964. Even this dream, shared by many, was suddenly shattered. As he rode through

Dallas, Texas, on November 22, 1963, waving to well wishers, he was shot down by rifle fire, the fourth President assassinated while in office. Millions of Americans were utterly stunned by this news they found hard to comprehend. Kennedy was given an impressive state funeral attended not only by a great mass of Americans but by leaders from foreign lands. Thus he passed from the national and international scene with the eyes of the world still focused on him, now remembered for his aspirations, his culture, and his enthusiasm, perhaps, more than for his lasting, concrete achievements.

LYNDON B. JOHNSON

★★

RIDING ONLY two cars behind Kennedy through the streets of Dallas, Texas, on November 22, 1963, Vice-President Lyndon B. Johnson could hear the shots that killed his chief. Within a few hours, he took the oath of office, and assumed command in the nation's capital before the day was over.

Strong and able in appearance, received with sympathy by a shocked nation, and familiar with the ways of Congress, Johnson soon put Kennedy's stalled legislative program in motion. One of his major achievements was getting through Congress sweeping civil rights laws, benefitting Negroes and other minority groups, and reducing job discrimination against women. For Johnson, himself a Southerner from Texas, to declare the cause of the Negro "must be our cause too" took high courage.

Johnson's proven ability to bring about the passage of such legislation in the few months that elapsed before the Democratic party held its next national convention in 1964 easily won for him its nomination for the presidency. His own selection of Hubert H. Humphrey, Jr., Senator from Minnesota, as his running mate was also quickly approved. Against this ticket the Republicans ran another man from the South-west, Senator Barry M. Goldwater of Arizona, a conservative advocating stronger military action in Vietnam. Johnson's "public image" proved strikingly popular, however. Emerging with an unprecedented mandate, over 61 per cent of the popular vote, and backed by an overwhelmingly Democratic Congress, Johnson opened his first full term as President in 1965 in a confident mood.

One of the most seasoned politicians in Washington, Johnson had spent most of his life preparing for such an opportunity. First appearing in the capital as secretary to a Democratic Congressman, he returned after the elections of 1936 as a Representative in Congress from Texas. Elevated to the Senate in 1949, he rose to the key post of Majority Leader. From this high base he sought the Democratic nomination for President in 1960 but, outmaneuvered by the powerful Kennedy forces, contented himself with the office of Vice-President. The doors of the White House were opened for him by the tragic events in Dallas and now he had received the most sweeping victory a candidate had ever won.

A tall Texan with his own cattle ranches, Johnson was one of our few landed Presidents. He brought to the Washington scene a Western air that had been absent since the days of Theodore Roosevelt and his Rough Riders. In other ways, too, he was a contrast to his predecessor: fifty-five years of age on taking office, he was much older than Kennedy, and had devoted over three decades to public service. Unlike Kennedy, he was a self-made man. Raised in straitened circumstances, he had worked his way through college and supported himself for a while by teaching. Later he had become a millionaire, with his wife's help, through successful business ventures that included radio and television stations.

Near the peak of his power in 1965, he went beyond the

earlier dreams of Democratic leaders, such as Roosevelt's "New Deal" and Kennedy's "New Frontiers," by calling for the creation of a "Great Society," to be built "in our cities, our countryside, and in our classrooms." He urged major legislative attacks on disease and poverty, on urban ills and the pollution of our air and water. He demanded a broad educational program and the promotion of the fine arts.

A firm believer in what he called a "consensus" of opinion, Johnson strove to unite many groups in improving the lives of the poor, the old, the sick, the young and disadvantaged. He believed that America, undergoing rapid change under the impact of advances in science, must prepare at once for the consequences. Johnson's programs, then, were not called forth primarily by a sudden crisis, like those of Roosevelt; they were more preventive, designed to smooth the passage of the United States into new roles as a leader among the great technological societies.

Congress and much of the nation went along at first with his thinking. Within a very short time, a remarkably wide range of bills were rushed through, creating a Poverty Program and a system of medical aid, extending federal help to education in new areas, establishing a Department of Transportation, promoting urban redevelopment, covering voting and housing discrimination and protecting consumers. In contrast with some 45 social programs operating under Eisenhower, over 400 were developing under Johnson.

Johnson thus left a deep imprint on American government and society in his slightly more than five years in office. Given his swift pace, his enormous energy and the wide support he had been able to muster, he left office with a feeling he had accomplished much for his country and established trends that would be hard to change. Then, just a few weeks before he left the White House, he had the satisfaction of watching, on television, three American astronauts make the first flight of human beings deep into outer space, an event that won respect around the globe.

Yet Johnson had his sorrows, too, as he admitted in his final address to Congress in January, 1969. His vast programs had been enormously expensive. They had been attended with much waste and confusion. The great expectations he had aroused had not been adequately fulfilled and instead of the "consensus" he had sought he had been plagued by angry "confrontations." Militant Negroes, impatient with their progress, had left a trail of riots, burned out buildings and looted stores. Despite heavy infusions of federal money into education, violence had become commonplace on school and college campuses. From coast to coast protestors, paraders and crippling strikes of teachers, policemen and firemen were disrupting order. Crime had been rising rapidly and the Supreme Court was being widely criticized for some of its decisions, which some thought impeded the work of the police. Monetary problems cropped up as the economy, over-heated at home and over-expanding abroad, was harassed by inflation, rising interest rates and balance of payments difficulties.

Above all, it was the increasingly unpopular struggle in Vietnam, that became the longest war in American history during his administration, which aroused antagonism against Johnson's leadership. He had fallen heir to the problems of jungle warfare which Eisenhower and Kennedy had been unable to solve. He had had to make the hard decision as to whether to pull out, dishonoring pledges and perhaps leaving all Asia open to Communist take-overs, or to throw ever more money and American troops into battle. Although he determined to fight, he ordered several lulls in aerial bombardment while he listened for peace offers from the Communists, and then resumed action. Meanwhile the bitter combat cost thousands of American lives. The public was less patient than Johnson with this seemingly endless war and many critics assailed him in terms of outrage that had not been used against a president since the days of Abraham Lincoln. Even his own party was torn apart by disputes over Vietnam.

Meanwhile, Johnson had intervened to put down disturbances in Santo Domingo and tried to avert the spread of Cuban-type Communism into Latin America. He reached an agreement with the Soviet Union on the use of arms in outer space; Russian leaders even sat down at a table with him in Glassboro, New Jersey, for a summit conference. But events abroad on many fronts had prevented Johnson from devoting as much money and effort as he would have liked to the further building of his Great Society at home.

As the opening of a new presidential campaign came, he made the sudden announcement, in March, 1968, that he would not seek another term. Before ending nearly four decades of public service in Washington, he said he would throw his energies into trying to bring about peace in Vietnam, rather than into election-year politics. He ordered a partial halt in the bombing of North Vietnam and almost on the eve of the elections in 1968 hopefully hinted that a break-through in peace negotiations was expected.

Peace could not be won so easily, however, and Johnson's failure here and his withdrawal from political leadership at home left his party in disarray. After so many years—all but 8 of the preceding 36—of Democratic rule, many factions had developed. One strong contender for the party's nomination, Robert Kennedy, a brother of the assassinated John F. Kennedy, was in his turn assassinated. Shortly afterward, Johnson's political heir, Vice-President Humphrey, faced a stormy Convention in 1968. Chosen by the Democrats to run against another experienced Vice-President, Richard M. Nixon, and encountering opposition from a new group, the American Independent Party led by George C. Wallace, Humphrey and his Democratic regulars lost the presidency, although the party remained in control of Congress.

RICHARD M. NIXON

★★★

AFTER EIGHT YEARS of dramatic change under two Democratic presidents, the voters placed a Republican in power in 1968. Nixon, a quiet man, made few big promises during his campaign. His inaugural address was mild. The new president, a Quaker, urged his countrymen to seek unity, to lower their voices and to "look within" for guidance.

He had learned patience the hard way. He had stood up under an unusual load of disappointment and gone through "the fires of defeat" to reach this hour when, as he put it, "the man and the moment in history" came together.

Reared in California—the first President born West of the Rockies—Nixon had a plain and poor background. He carried the double burden of schoolwork and chores in his father's grocery. Graduating from the Quaker Whittier College, he won a scholarship to a Southern law school. Returning from World War II as a Lieutenant Commander in the Navy, he entered politics, serving in both houses of Congress.

Barely forty when he became Vice-President under Eisenhower, Nixon soon went abroad to treat with foreign leaders, learning much about the world, and at home he dealt with Congress and the Cabinet. Capitalizing on this unusual background, he sought the presidency in 1960 but lost to Kennedy by the slimmest margin in over fifty years. Later, he was defeated for the Governorship of California.

Despite these setbacks, Nixon refused to quit. Starting over, he gained new political influence by hard work for his party, and through legal practice and Florida real estate acquired a modest fortune. His efforts brought results. In 1968 the Republicans backed him for president against Democrat Hubert H. Humphrey, Jr. and Independent George C. Wallace. While none of these three self-made men from small towns generated great enthusiasm, Nixon's persistence paid off. Winning forty-four per cent of the vote, he entered the White House, the first to get there on a second try in over seventy-five years.

At once he opened a "new era of negotiations," encouraging nations to discuss differences rather than fight over them. His main goal was what he called "peace with honor," a ceasefire in Southeast Asia that would give our allies some protection, weak though it might turn out to be, instead of leaving them at the mercy of the enemy.

Achieving it was discouragingly slow. As months dragged by, exasperated "doves" at home and abroad called for a swift and complete pullout from Southeast Asia, regardless of the consequences. There were numerous anti-war demonstrations, some violent. On top of all this, work on secret negotiations with the enemy was set back in March, 1972, when the North Vietnamese launched a major offensive into South Vietnam. Nixon retaliated by ordering a heavy aerial bombardment of the North and the mining of its harbors to halt delivery of war supplies by sea, to prevent an enemy military victory. He was then assailed at home for undertaking a dangerous venture. Throughout his first term, peace remained a mere hope.

Yet major progress was being made in other directions. Starting in June, 1969, he "Vietnamized" the war by shifting more and more of the ground fighting to native troops, strengthened by American air power and lots of American supplies. Soldiers thus released were brought home in stages, cutting the American commitment in Vietnam from over half a million men when he took office to less than 40,000 by Election Day, 1972.

Meanwhile he tried to improve American relations with the two major Communist powers, Red China and Russia, who had given the North Vietnamese most of their war supplies and moral support. He had prestige, grain for their hungry millions hit by drought, and other favors to offer in return for a softening of their stands on the war.

Shortly after the withdrawal of American opposition enabled Red China to join the United Nations, Nixon was invited to Peking. In February, 1972, as the first American president ever to visit the world's most populous nation, he relaxed some old tensions and opened the path for an exchange of ideas, people and trade. Three months later he was in Moscow, conferring with Russian leaders in a similar goodwill tour. Soon American wheat was cleared for shipment there, a nuclear weapons agreement was developed and America, which under Nixon had put the first humans in history on the moon, had offered to make a joint space flight with the Russians. With the cold war on the wane, Nixon's exclusion of Russian and Chinese ships from the mined harbors of Vietnam brought only verbal protests.

To the unrest generated at home by the war were added domestic worries: crime, drug abuse, air and water pollution, mounting food costs and a growing scarcity of jobs. Young people criticized "the establishment" and gained the vote for eighteen-year-olds. Militant women pushed for state ratification of the equal rights amendment to the constitution. Ethnic groups complained of discrimination. Tempers grew over the busing of school children. Nixon often relied on his Vice-President, Spiro Agnew, a southerner of Greek-American background, to take on his critics, charging them with representing small groups and arguing that the "quiet majority" of "middle Americans" backed the president.

There was something in Agnew's theory. Nearly all factions, both capital and labor, peacefully accepted the ninety-day freeze on wages, prices and rents imposed by Nixon on August 15, 1971, to stop runaway inflation. They even accepted his subsequent period of federal wage and price regulation with reasonable calm.

Meanwhile excessive pile ups of American dollars in foreign lands—from imports, the stationing of troops overseas and other causes—was producing a fall in the value of the dollar relative to foreign currency. Forced to cope with this emergency, Nixon ended the exchange of even foreign-held dollars for gold, thus taking the country entirely off the gold standard, and accepted a considerable reduction in the exchange rate for American money.

In a further move to combat inflation, Nixon tried to hold down or cut back on various expensive federal programs. However, with a Congress controlled by Democrats and under pressure from local constituents, his influence was limited. Besides he wasn't always frugal himself—he signed a bill raising social security checks twenty per cent almost on the eve of the 1972 elections.

While it could not be said that at the end of his first term Nixon was overwhelmingly popular, the Democrats failed to pick a convincing candidate to run against him. Old leaders faltered and a new man, George S. McGovern, seized the reins of the party under novel rules that packed the 1972 convention with a majority of newcomers, including young people, women, minority group members and war protestors, all foreign to party regulars. He proposed reforms radical even to Democrats and promised a quick end to the war in Vietnam with little consideration for our allies. Democrats in droves flocked to Nixon's aid, in both the South and the North. Nixon hardly budged from his office and said little. McGovern flew about the country hurling harsh accusations. At the close of this strange campaign Nixon had 97 per cent of the electoral votes.

Shortly after his second inaugural, Nixon ended American combat operations in the nation's longest war, that in Vietnam, and brought troops and newly released prisoners of war home. Then in June, 1973, Soviet party chief Leonid Brezhnev's visit to the United States seemed to signal the close of an even longer contest, the so-called "Cold War" between the East and the West. The new relaxed relationship helped Nixon arrange a cease-fire in 1974, between Arab and Israeli forces, on Russia's Near Eastern doorstep, that affected America's oil supply.

Meanwhile Nixon's hopes for being remembered for his successes abroad were being dimmed by reversals at home. His administration, members of his staff, and some of his friends in private life were charged with acts forbidden by law. The scandals ranged from attempting to cover up the use of Republican funds, to financing a break-in at the Watergate headquarters of the Democratic National Committee in the 1972 campaign, to tapping wires and collecting campaign funds in illegal ways. Some cabinet members quit, a few of Nixon's former subordinates were jailed and Vice President Agnew resigned under fire.

With Agnew's resignation, Nixon was obligated, under the Twenty-Fifth Amendment to the Constitution, to choose a successor for confirmation by Congress. Nixon offered one of his loyal Republican supporters, Gerald R. Ford, to the Democratically-controlled Congress, which then subjected the nominee to a very intensive investigation. Satisfied that he had not been a party to the Watergate or any other scandal, Congress confirmed Ford by large majorities in both houses. Shortly afterward, he took the oath of office as Vice President. Given the uncertainty at the time over what might happen to Nixon, Congress and the country now felt greatly relieved.

While many feared Nixon might be deeply involved in the scandals he denied it and clung tenaciously to his post, declaring he owed it to the public that had elected him to complete his term. He also pointed out that yielding ground under pressure from Congress and the courts would weaken the office of president and handicap future Chief Executives. In particular he argued that a president enjoys the "executive privilege" of preserving the secrecy of tape recordings made by him at the White House of frank discussions of public affairs.

After months of charges, countercharges, and investigation, the struggle between the executive and the legislative and judicial branches of the government reached the decisive stage. On July 24, 1974, the Supreme Court unanimously ordered Nixon to release 64 tapes of his intimate conversations to a federal judge. Although recognizing that there was such a thing as "executive privilege," the Court ruled it was not so broad as to prevent a judge from inspecting tapes needed in a criminal trial. Six days later attention shifted to the House Judiciary Committee which, for the first time since charges were made against President Andrew Johnson in 1868, recommended a presidential impeachment, that of Nixon. Shortly after the Committee's action, Nixon released the contents of a court-ordered tape which indicated the Committee had correctly claimed he had been involved in the Watergate cover-up.

Finally, insiders told Nixon his supporters were turning away, and that if he tried to remain in power he would probably not only be impeached by the House but tried and removed by the Senate. So Nixon made a hard decision. On the night of August 8, 1974, in a nation-wide telecast, without mentioning the word "impeachment" or specifically admitting involvement in the Watergate affair, Nixon acknowledged that he had lost his "political base" in Congress and that he had decided, in the "interests of America," to give up the fight to keep his office. The next day he became the first president in American history to resign.

Extraordinary by American standards, his resignation was something less than that by world standards. In 1974 alone, for example, no-confidence votes overturned administrations in Canada, and Great Britain, and Willy Brandt, Chancellor of West Germany, resigned over a spy scandal. Even dictatorships in Greece and Portugal were broken. With Nixon's action, America had merely lost its historic immunity to the kind of instability that had long plagued other lands.

Shortly after his resignation, Nixon was given a pardon by his successor, President Ford. It was so worded as to prevent the trial of Nixon in court for "offenses against the United States which he has committed or may have committed or taken part in" during his term of office. It did not say whether in fact he had violated any law. In accepting the pardon, the only light Nixon shed on the controversy was that "the way" he had tried to deal with the Watergate affair had been "the wrong way." Then he settled down at his California home to work on his memoirs.

Gerald R. Ford

GERALD R. FORD

★★

WHEN Vice President Gerald R. Ford became President on August 9, 1974, following Richard Nixon's resignation earlier that day, the country acquired for the first time a Chief Executive of unknown popularity. Unlike all his predecessors, Ford had never run for the presidency, or the vice-presidency that can lead to it, in a national election (see p. 165). In his first telecast, Ford appealed to his audience to "confirm" him with its prayers.

The new president had been born in Omaha, Nebraska, in 1913, and named Leslie King, Jr. At the age of two his parents were divorced. Shortly afterward his mother married a salesman, Gerald R. Ford, who adopted the boy and renamed him Gerald R. Ford, Jr. Brought up in Grand Rapids, Michigan, he learned the importance of hard work and honesty and made a name for himself in football. Later he earned his way through the law school at Yale as a member of the University's athletic staff.

After practicing law and rising in the Naval Reserve during World War II to the rank of Lieutenant Commander, Ford turned to a political career. It began in 1948 with his election as a Representative from his home district in Michigan.

Through repeated re-elections and capable work, he rose to the rank of Republican minority leader in the House, from which position he was elevated to the vice-presidency, his stepping stone to the White House.

Such was the man who on August 9, 1974, inherited both Nixon's job and the problems of his administration. One of the most pressing of these carry-overs was the Watergate scandal. Instead of wasting any more valuable time dealing with it in court, Ford, on September 8, 1974, freed himself for more constructive work by pardoning Nixon in the manner described in the preceding chapter. Many viewed this as a statesmanlike means of getting on with his job. It was, however, politically risky, for many Americans considered the pardon itself to be "unpardonable." Through it, for the first time, an ex-president had been placed substantially above the law. Resentments so generated lingered on, contributing to Ford's own downfall two years later.

In a few months more, another major inherited problem, the collapse of Nixon's peace settlement for Southeast Asia, began to solve itself, as communist forces from North Vietnam launched a massive offensive to the south. Since Congress had previously forbidden stopping it with American troops and native resistance crumbled, the advance was swift. In April, 1975, the communists overran Cambodia, then South Vietnam. Before the year was out Laos also fell. Thus America's long, frustrating and expensive efforts to carry out its policies in this part of Asia came to an inglorious end.

When dealing with foreign affairs elsewhere, Ford avoided applying pressures that might throw American troops back into combat, and resorted to negotiations instead. In the Near East, where Arab nations armed with Soviet weapons threatened the existence of Israel, he approved the peace-keeping Sinai agreement. Traveling in person to Japan, China, and the Soviet Union, he tried personal diplomacy. Then at Helsinki,

Finland, he signed a multi-national agreement for Europe placing at least some moral obligations on the Soviet Union.

In this relatively peaceful setting Ford was free to devote a lot of attention to domestic matters, including what he called the number one problem of inflation. Faced with an annual rise in the cost of living of over 11 percent shortly after taking office, Ford tried to reduce it by cutting federal spending. He pleaded with the Democratically-controlled Congress to trim the cost of a number of its programs. When it refused he successfully vetoed some of the laws involved. By late 1976 he had the satisfaction of seeing the rate of inflation greatly reduced.

Meanwhile, business slowed down severely in 1975, bringing the rate of unemployment to the highest level in over three decades. Here again Ford urged remedial action, such as the granting of tax incentives to business. Some revival of business and a reduction in unemployment followed.

As he neared the end of his temporary presidency, Ford entered the election of 1976, hoping to gain widespread popular support. His efforts, however, were in trouble from the start. Rivalry within his own party produced so much dissension at its 1976 National Convention that Ford just barely won the Republican nomination. As is customary, he was also blamed for the sluggishness of the business recovery and the still relatively high rate of unemployment as election day neared. Alternating between trying to do a forceful job as President in Washington and rushing out into the field to shore up his campaign, Ford lost by a narrow margin to the remarkably determined Democratic opponent, Jimmy Carter. Thus Ford became the nation's first purely nonelected president and the second fallen Republican in a row.

JAMES E. CARTER

★★

T HE troubles that had come upon the Republicans during the Nixon and Ford administrations left their party disorganized. While this heartened the Democrats, their own leadership was weak and confused. With both parties in disarray, it remained for a newcomer, James Earl Carter, Jr., to seize the golden chance and make a direct appeal to the public.

Carter had never served in Washington as a congressman or in any major federal administrative post, as most previous presidents had done. Indeed, his first aim in life had not been political. Born in Plains, Georgia, in 1924, he worked on his father's farm while dreaming of a naval career. His father, an officer in World War I, helped him to enter Annapolis during World War II as a naval cadet. After graduating, he served as an officer assigned to engineering duties such as the nuclear-powered submarine program.

Finding advancement slow in peacetime, Carter left the Navy after his father's death, returned to Plains, and went into business for himself. He developed farming and related peanut warehousing enterprises that provided him with a substantial fortune. It enabled him to enter local Democratic politics. After winning two terms in the Georgia Senate, he became governor of his state.

Georgia was then a prospering region of the so-called "New South." Industry and the spirit of enterprise had replaced the old apathy born of defeat in the Civil War. Local businessmen were pleased when Carter led trade missions abroad to promote Georgia's products. They backed his presidential aims, acquired in 1972 as governor, because they wanted to see a southerner again in the White House.

However, Carter was relatively unknown—an outsider without powerful connections in the national party. It was a daring gamble for him to enter the race. In 1976, backed by a private campaign group, he set forth on long hard journeys to thirty states to meet voters in person in advance of the party caucuses and primaries. No other candidate had traveled so far or worked so hard for this purpose before. He extended his hand everywhere with a smile, saying to strangers, "Hello, I'm Jimmy Carter and I'm running for president." Newspapers spread the story of this self-made politician and his unusual campaign, winning him sympathy. Carter not only swept the caucuses and primaries but the Democratic National Convention of that year as well, to the astonishment of professional politicians.

He now had an organization behind him but little money. Fortunately he soon received, under a new law, his share of the federal funds given to both major presidential candidates for their final campaigning. Because both parties were in confusion, he persuaded large numbers of voters to cross lines—political and sectional. Many Blacks, traditionally Republican, voted for the Democrat who seemed to offer brighter prospects. Carter appealed to women, labor leaders, and minorities with sweeping promises, expressing his idealism and compassion.

When he won the election, however, and came to Washington with a small band of loyal followers from Georgia, he faced grave problems at home ranging from inflation to a rapidly rising national debt. Unrest abroad and an arms race with the Soviet Union endangered the position of the United States. Being a stranger to Washington, Carter was too inexperienced to deal with all these matters effectively alone. He needed the cooperation of many others, including the largely Democratic Congress, but failed to approach such people soon enough to make smooth progress. He did not even bother to rebuild his own party.

For this and other reasons, Carter failed to meet some important goals that he had set for himself when running for president. He never balanced the budget, for example, although in his 1976 campaign he had promised to see that the federal government lived within its means. Nor was the annual rate of inflation cut to the low 4 percent he had said the country could expect. Instead, the rate was over three times higher in 1980, his last year in office. In the presence of such failures, many people overlooked his accomplishments: from reducing American dependence on foreign oil to giving women and minorities more important positions in the government.

At first, his administration had some successes in foreign affairs. He called for peace, limitation of armaments, and a new world order based on the doctrine of basic human rights, a concept with a great appeal. He was able to persuade Congress to arrange for turning the Panama Canal over to the Panamanian government, and he brought two bitter enemies, Egypt and Israel, together in a temporary accord. Following Nixon's lead, he completed recognition of communist mainland China, though he cast aside an old ally, Taiwan, in the process.

Then, the Senate refused to ratify an arms limitation treaty with the Soviet Union negotiated by his administration. A revolution broke out in Iran and its ruler, the Shah, who had been friendly to the United States fled from the country. Later, members of the American Embassy in Iran were seized and held as hostages, contrary to international law.

Carter's dream of establishing harmony in the world was

shaken even more when Soviet troops invaded the independent nation of Afghanistan. A war broke out in the oil-rich region of the Middle East between Iraq and Iran that he couldn't halt. In an effort to get the Soviet Union to pull its troops out of Afghanistan, Carter protested against their presence, embargoed grain shipments to Russia, and asked American athletes not to compete in the Olympic Games held in Moscow, but to no avail.

As his troubles increased, the confidence of voters in Carter's administration declined. Opinion polls, which came to play a greater role in politics, showed Carter was widely viewed as a weak leader. With the 1980 election drawing near, he took a daring gamble. Since the plight of the American hostages in Iran had aroused the sympathy of the American people, he secretly sent a small task force into Iran at night to release them. After some losses of both aircraft and men, they pulled out in defeat before dawn without bringing back any hostages. The poor quality of American military equipment and planning was made painfully plain, and Carter's political future was endangered by that disaster in the desert. To make matters even worse, although he negotiated for the release of the hostages later, they did not actually leave Iran until minutes after his term of office expired.

Amid threats abroad and uneasiness at home caused by increasing inflation and unemployment, Carter faced a challenge at the polls by a man who resembled him in many ways, Ronald W. Reagan. Reagan had also risen from obscurity to be a governor; he was also a stranger to Washington at the time he ran for president. Unlike Carter, Reagan did not need to make hard journeys to speak to voters in remote places. Reagan was a master of television, the art of reaching vast audiences, which was increasing in importance as a media.

The campaign aroused little enthusiasm. The voters showed

apathy until, at the last moment, after a televised debate between Carter and Reagan, a sudden tide rose for the Republican candidate. Georgia remained faithful to Carter, but he
lost nearly every other state. Carter went down as dramatically
as he had risen.

Ronald Reagan

RONALD W. REAGAN

★★★

A PPROACHING seventy, Ronald Reagan was in 1981 the oldest man so far to become president. However, he understood the demands in the modern political arena better than many younger people. He had grown up working in many channels of communication—radio, cinema, and television—before, late in life, bursting into politics.

A small-town boy, he was born in an apartment over a general store on Main Street, Tampico, Illinois, in 1911. He spent his youth in prairie towns and villages. Later, he won a scholarship to small, nearby, Eureka College, where he was active in football and dramatics. At twenty-one, he broke into the growing field of radio, having a good baritone voice, and became a sportscaster. Attracted to the expanding movie industry, he became a Hollywood star, though not a famous one. His career was interrupted by World War II, and he found another avenue of expression as host of a television show sponsored by a large industrial corporation.

Television had already made its mark on the elections of 1960 during the Nixon-Kennedy debate. Four years later, a powerful speech by Reagan was televised on his show, which raised millions of dollars for the Republican presidential candidate in 1964, again demonstrating the force of this medium.

Stirred by his success, a group of California businessmen urged Reagan to run as a Republican for the governorship of that predominantly Democratic state. With surprising ease, he won two terms in a row, using the media and calling himself a "citizen-politician."

He was already well into his fifties when he became governor. Over thirty years of his life had been spent in show business. But he had been more than a performer; he had learned much about industry and politics while presiding over the many local branches of the Screen Actors Guild. While a television host, he had been sent to numerous factory towns and chambers of commerce to speak on economic and political issues. He turned from the Democratic loyalties of his father to a more conservative outlook as a Republican.

While serving as a successful governor of California, Reagan was tempted by friends, mostly industrialists, to aim for a higher office. In 1968, still too busy with administration to devote himself freely to the enterprise, Reagan offered himself as the Republican presidential alternative to Nixon and lost. Then, with more time available, he ran against Ford in 1976 and almost won the Republican nomination. Finally, in 1980, he became his party's candidate and could face Carter with all the skills he had acquired.

Speeches and debates, nationally televised, did much to win voters for Reagan. However, more important to Reagan's victory were the factors of a worsening economy, mounting inflation, and the evident weaknesses of the United States in dealing with threats to its leadership abroad. A rising tide of conservative feeling not only carried him into office, but gave the Republicans their first majority in the Senate in twenty-six years and increased their representation in the House and among state governors. This swing in popular mood aided Reagan in his first efforts to reform the government.

Under Reagan, the isolation of the White House from Congress was ended. The president, in an unusual gesture of friendliness, went to the Capitol to pay calls even on his Democratic opponents and invited members of Congress to talks in the White House in an effort to gain strong backing for his policies.

In response to the Soviet Union's arms buildup and its support of communist governments and guerrillas in other countries, Reagan persuaded Congress to authorize increased United States military spending, development of new weapon systems, and delivery of arms to allies. Under his administration, presumed threats to the security of the United States and its allies were met with strong shows of force in Lebanon, Grenada, and Central America. At home, he began broad economic changes, including transfer of federal obligations back to the individual states and revitalization of the economy through tax cuts, federal deregulation of business, and reduced spending on welfare and other domestic service programs.

Although the president had numerous achievements to his credit, he did help create some major problems. United States marines in Lebanon, open targets for terrorists, were the victims of a severe attack. Imports exceeded exports by record numbers, harming American industries and their employees. Increased spending, especially for the military, helped keep the federal budget unbalanced, and the national debt grew to an alarming figure—an all-time high of more than a trillion dollars.

Despite the difficulties of his first term as president, Reagan asked for more time and got it. Running against the badly divided Democrats in the 1984 election, he won a second term by the largest majority of electoral votes in forty-eight years. With this strong support, he began his new term with an air of confidence.

The second term of the Reagan administration witnessed the loss of some of the glamour surrounding the first. This was partly because of the inevitable loss of novelty in a second term and partly because of the substitution of a set of administrators in the White House less deft than those who had handled affairs in the first four years. The scandal known as the Iran-Contra affair involved attempts to trade arms for hostages with Iran, even when we were urging an international boycott of that hostile state. The proceeds from those trades were used to provide support for the so-called Contra forces fighting the government of Nicaragua in the face of congressional denial of funds to the group. Although public opinion concluded that Reagan had not himself directed these operations, there was a general sense that his "hands-off" attitude toward the details of governing was itself a source of problems. Insensitivity on the part of various presidential appointees to the ethical obligations of holders of high office further shadowed Reagan's image. Still, Reagan's personal popularity continued to be high, and he left office with the highest approval rating of any president since Eisenhower.

GEORGE HERBERT WALKER BUSH

★★

Few presidents have come to that office with the wide experience of high-level public service that George Bush
brought to the post. Despite that, it was hard for observers in
early 1989 to understand what this former Vice President's
own policies, programs, and style might be as President.

Bush was born in Milton, Massachusetts, on June 12, 1924,
the son of Prescott Bush, at one time a U.S. Senator. Serving
as a naval aviator during World War II, he was shot down over
the Pacific and earned several decorations. He returned home
to marry Barbara Pierce in 1945 and then to graduate from
Yale College. He moved from New England to Texas, where he
entered the oil business, cofounding the Zapata Petroleum
Corporation. He then turned his interests to Texas politics,
serving two terms as a member of the House of Representatives (1967-71), but was unsuccessful in two bids for the U.S.
Senate, one in 1964 and one in 1970. His winning opponent in
1970 was Lloyd Bentsen, who became the vice presidential
candidate on the Democratic team that opposed Bush in 1988.
Bush's efforts for the Republican party in Texas brought him
to the attention of President Nixon, who entrusted him with a
series of important positions at the national level. Bush served as

ambassador to the United Nations and then as Chairman of the Republican National Committee. Bush next represented this country in Beijing at a time when we were just starting to build relations with the People's Republic of China. In 1976 he was asked to become director of the Central Intelligence Agency, which had just gone through a difficult period. Each of these positions was an important and useful one, but none of them enabled Bush to stake out an independent position as policy-maker or to project a clear image.

In 1980 Bush campaigned for the Republican nomination for President. Beaten in that contest by Ronald Reagan, he accepted the vice presidential nomination and campaigned loyally for the ticket. He then served for eight years as Vice President, participating in the inner councils of the administration and carrying out missions for the President. It was hard for anybody outside of the administration to make out what role he played in its processes. Although he had been critical of aspects of Reagan's policies during the 1980 primaries, labeling part of them as "voodoo economics," he made no independent gestures during those eight years. In particular, it remained obscure what role he had played during the Iran-Contra maneuvers of 1985–1986.

The 1988 campaign brought little clarification regarding Bush's stands on the major questions of the time. His choice of a relatively unknown senator, Dan Quayle of Indiana, as his running mate puzzled many. A cleverly run campaign concentrated on the vulnerabilities of his Democratic opponent, Governor Michael Dukakis of Massachusetts, attacking him for liberalism, for being soft on crime, and for his willingness to spend and tax. Campaign promises were few and vague, with the exception of a repeated pledge not to raise new taxes. Many wondered what to make, in the midst of a rather vicious campaign, of a pledge to create a kinder and gentler society.

In his first months of office Bush faced a variety of challenges left by Ronald Reagan. He faced them in the company of a Congress, in both houses, controlled by the Democratic party. The challenges related partly to the economy, which, although it continued to be prosperous, was viewed with varying degrees of alarm by economists because of the vast and increasing annual budget deficits and total federal debt, the continuing failure of our exports to match our imports, and the growing indebtedness of the United States to other countries. Whether a selective, flexible freeze on government spending could solve these problems, as Bush indicated, seemed highly questionable to many.

The other major challenge related to foreign policy. The sharply revised policies of the Soviet Union, characterized as *glasnost* (openness) and *perestroika* (restructuring), posed both opportunities and threats to U.S. foreign policy. On the one hand, Mikhail Gorbachev offered opportunities for a reduction of tensions between the two countries that had caused the "cold war." This change could lead to new openings for advantageous economic relations and consequently major savings through armaments reductions. On the other hand, if we let down our guard prematurely we might lose the initiative to the impressively bold operations of Gorbachev.

A variety of social issues at home also challenged the new president; they involved the growing threat of drugs to the fabric of American society, the passionately debated issue of abortion, and other problems relating to family life and the malaise in the American educational system.

In any case, his inaugural address was conciliatory and made a strong plea for cooperation and responsibility; the image he projected in the midst of his large and harmonious family was appealing. Fortunately, the mood of Congress and the American people seemed to be one of willingness to give President Bush a fair chance to lead us in tackling our problems.

BIOGRAPHICAL DIGEST

★★

Numbering the Presidents. The numbers preceding the names of the Presidents in the headings below show the order in which they took their turns in office. While it is customary to use these figures to number the Presidents as well, this system has one drawback. As Cleveland's two terms were separated by the administration of Benjamin Harrison, Cleveland thereby becomes both the twenty-second and the twenty-fourth President. Can *one man* actually be *two different Presidents?* Truman thought not. After being listed as the thirty-third President in the above manner, he argued that as the thirty-second *man* to hold the post, he could only be the thirty-second President.

"Conflicting" Dates. The dates given below are in the "New Style," based on the accurate Gregorian Calendar now in general use. Omitted here, but sometimes seen in other works, are their "Old Style" equivalents, derived from the defective Julian Calendar which British America did not officially abandon until September 14, 1752. Thus George Washington's birth date, written below in the New Style as February 22, 1732, appears in the family Bible as February 11, 1731—its Old Style equivalent.

Public Careers. A convenient way to study the careers of the Presidents is to read their lives in the authoritative *Dictionary of American Biography*, then consult the works about them listed in these accounts.

The Cabinet. The "Cabinet" consists of certain high officials who carry out the President's major policies and who meet frequently with him as a group. Besides the members listed below (almost exclusively department heads) others have sometimes attended Cabinet meetings.

The Vote. The Constitution (Article II, Section 2; Twelfth Amendment) provides for the indirect choice of the President by a small number of "Electors" or, in case they are unable to settle the matter, by the House of Representatives.

By 1836, however, the practice of having ordinary voters choose Electors pledged in advance to favor specific candidates had become almost universal. So figures on this popular vote have been included below—for the election of that year and all subsequent elections.

1 GEORGE WASHINGTON

Born: February 22, 1732 in Westmoreland County, Va.

Died: December 14, 1799, at Mount Vernon, Va. Buried: Mt. Vernon, Va.

Married: Martha Dandridge Custis (1732–1802) in 1759.

Public Career: Major of Militia, Colonel; Member of Continental Congress; Commander-in-Chief of Army; President of Constitutional Convention.

Presidential Terms: 1789–97.

Vice-President: John Adams.

CABINET

Secretary of State—John Jay (*acting*) 1789; Thomas Jefferson 1789–94; Edmund Randolph 1794–95; Timothy Pickering 1795–97.

Secretary of the Treasury—Alexander Hamilton 1789–95; Oliver Wolcott 1795–97.

Secretary of War—Henry Knox 1789–95; Timothy Pickering 1795–96; James McHenry 1796–97.

Attorney General [1]—Edmund Randolph 1789–94; William Bradford 1794–95; Charles Lee 1795–97.

Postmaster General [1]—Samuel Osgood 1789–91; Timothy Pickering 1791–95; Joseph Habersham 1795–97.

[1] The offices of Attorney General and Postmaster General were created by Congress in 1789, but the Attorney General was not made a full-fledged cabinet member until 1814, the Postmaster General until 1829.

VOTE

1789	*Electoral Vote*
George Washington	69[1]
John Adams	34
John Jay	9
1792	
George Washington (Federalist [2])	132
John Adams (Federalist)	77
George Clinton (Republican [2])	50

2 JOHN ADAMS

Born: October 30, 1735, at Braintree, Mass.
Died: July 4, 1826, at Quincy, Mass. Buried: Quincy, Mass.
Married: Abigail Smith (1744–1818) in 1764.
Public Career: Member of Continental Congress; Minister to England; Vice-President.
Presidential Term: 1797–1801.
Vice-President: Thomas Jefferson.

CABINET

Secretary of State—Timothy Pickering 1797–1800; John Marshall 1800–01.
Secretary of the Treasury—Oliver Wolcott 1797–1800; Samuel Dexter 1800–1801.
Secretary of War—James McHenry 1797–1800; Samuel Dexter 1800.
Attorney General—Charles Lee.
Postmaster General—Joseph Habersham.
Secretary of the Navy—Benjamin Stoddert.

[1] The Constitution originally provided that electors cast their votes for two persons, the one receiving the most votes becoming President, the one next becoming Vice-President. In 1789 and 1792, George Washington was considered elected unanimously since *all* electors cast one ballot for him, whereas their second votes were divided. As Adams received the most second votes he was elected Vice-President.

[2] Political parties did not exist in the first election, but by 1792 the first groupings were being formulated. Federalists, in the main, supported a strong national government and represented commercial interests; the Republican Party, the direct ancestor of the present Democratic Party, supported State's Rights and represented agricultural interests. (The word "Democratic" was, in the early days of the new nation, a word that struck fear in the hearts of many people.)

VOTE

1796	*Electoral Vote*	
John Adams (Federalist)	71	(became President)
Thomas Jefferson (Republican)	68	(became Vice-President)
Thomas Pinckney (Federalist)	59	

3 THOMAS JEFFERSON

Born: April 13, 1743, at Shadwell, Va.

Died: July 4, 1826, at Monticello, Va. Buried: Monticello, Va.

Married: Martha Wayles Skelton (1748–82) in 1772.

Public Career: Legislator; twice Continental Congressman; twice Assemblyman; Governor of Virginia; Minister to France; Secretary of State; Vice-President.

Presidential Terms: 1801–09.

Vice-President: Aaron Burr 1801–05; George Clinton 1805–09.

CABINET

Secretary of State—James Madison.

Secretary of the Treasury—Samuel Dexter 1801; Albert Gallatin 1801–09.

Secretary of War—Henry Dearborn.

Attorney General—Levi Lincoln 1801–05; Robert Smith 1805; John Breckenridge 1805–07; Caesar A. Rodney 1807–09.

Postmaster General—Joseph Habersham 1801; Gideon Granger 1801–09.

Secretary of the Navy—Benjamin Stoddert 1801; Robert Smith 1801–09.

VOTE

1800 [1]	*Electoral Vote*
Thomas Jefferson (Republican)	73
Aaron Burr (Republican)	73
John Adams (Federalist)	65
Charles C. Pinckney (Federalist)	64
1804 [1]	
Thomas Jefferson (Republican)	162
Charles C. Pinckney (Federalist)	14

[1] Since Jefferson and Burr were tied, the choice devolved upon the House of Representatives. Jefferson received votes of ten states, which made him President; Burr received four, which made him Vice-President. There were two blank votes. In 1804, the constitution having been amended, the electors voted for a President and a Vice-President.

4 JAMES MADISON

Born: March 16, 1751, at Port Conway, Va.
Died: June 28, 1836, at Montpelier, Va. Buried: Montpelier, Va.
Married: Dolly Payne Todd (1768–1849) in 1794.
Public Career: Assemblyman; Member of Continental Congress;
  Congressman; Secretary of State.
Presidential Terms: 1809–17.
Vice-Presidents: George Clinton 1809–12; Elbridge Gerry 1813–
  14.

CABINET

Secretary of State—Robert Smith 1809–11; James Monroe 1811–
  17.
Secretary of the Treasury—Albert Gallatin 1809–14; George W.
  Campbell 1814; Alexander J. Dallas 1814–16; Wm. H. Craw-
  ford 1816–17.
Secretary of War—William Eustis 1809–13; John Armstrong
  1813–14; James Monroe 1814–15; Wm. H. Crawford 1815–17.
Attorney General—Caesar A. Rodney 1809–11; William Pinkney
  1811–14; Richard Rush 1814–17.
Postmaster General—Gideon Granger 1809–14; Return J. Meigs,
  Jr. 1814–17.
Secretary of the Navy—Paul Hamilton 1809–13; William Jones
  1813–14; B. W. Crowninshield 1814–17.

VOTE

1808	Electoral Vote
James Madison (Republican)	122
Charles C. Pinckney (Federalist)	47
1812	
James Madison (Republican)	128
DeWitt Clinton (Federalist)	89

5 JAMES MONROE

Born: April 28, 1758, in Westmoreland County, Va.
Died: July 4, 1831, at New York City. Buried: Richmond, Va.
Married: Elizabeth Kortright (1768–1830) in 1786.
Public Career: Member of Virginia Legislature; Member of Con-
  tinental Congress; U. S. Senator; Minister to France, Spain, and
  England; Governor of Virginia; Secretary of State and of War.
Presidential Terms: 1817–25.
Vice-President: Daniel D. Tompkins.

CABINET

Secretary of State—John Quincy Adams.
Secretary of the Treasury—William H. Crawford.
Secretary of War—George Graham (*acting*) 1817; John C. Calhoun 1817–25.
Attorney General—Richard Rush 1817; William Wirt 1817–25.
Postmaster General—Return J. Meigs, Jr. 1817–23; John McLean 1823–25.
Secretary of the Navy—B. W. Crowninshield 1817–18; Smith Thompson 1818–23; Samuel L. Southard 1823–25.

VOTE

1816	Electoral Vote
James Monroe (Republican)	183
Rufus King (Federalist)	34
1820 [1]	
James Monroe (Republican)	231
John Quincy Adams (Republican)	1

6 JOHN QUINCY ADAMS

Born: July 11, 1767, at Braintree, Mass.
Died: February 23, 1848, at Washington, D. C. Buried: Quincy, Mass.
Married: Louisa Johnson (1775–1852) in 1797.
Public Career: Minister to Holland; Minister to Prussia; Member of Massachusetts Senate; U. S. Senator; Minister to Russia; Peace Commissioner at Ghent; Minister to England; Secretary of State; Congressman.
Presidential Term: 1825–29.
Vice-President: John C. Calhoun.

CABINET

Secretary of State—Henry Clay.
Secretary of the Treasury—Richard Rush.
Secretary of War—James Barbour 1825–28; Peter B. Porter 1828–29.
Attorney General—William Wirt.
Postmaster General—John McLean.
Secretary of the Navy—Samuel L. Southard.

[1] By 1820 the Federalist Party was almost extinct, so there was no real opposition to Monroe; one vote was cast for J. Q. Adams, leaving Washington as the only President ever elected unanimously.

VOTE

1824 [1]	*Electoral Vote*
Andrew Jackson	99
John Quincy Adams	84
William H. Crawford	41
Henry Clay	37

7 ANDREW JACKSON

Born: March 15, 1767, at Waxhaw, S. C.
Died: June 8, 1845, at Hermitage, Tenn. Buried: Hermitage, Tenn.
Married: Rachel Donelson Robards (1767–1828) in 1791.
Public Career: Congressman; Judge, Supreme Court of Tennessee; Major-General; Governor of Florida; U. S. Senator.
Presidential Terms: 1829–37.
Vice-Presidents: John C. Calhoun 1829–32; Martin Van Buren 1833–37.

CABINET

Secretary of State—Martin Van Buren 1829–31; Edward Livingston 1831–33; Louis McLane 1833–34; John Forsyth 1834–37.
Secretary of the Treasury—Samuel D. Ingham 1829–31; Louis McLane 1831–33; William J. Duane 1833; Roger B. Taney 1833–34; Levi Woodbury 1834–37.
Secretary of War—John H. Eaton 1829–31; Lewis Cass 1831–37; Benjamin F. Butler 1837.

[1] All candidates called themselves Republicans, as no other party existed; but splits were developing, leading to new party alignments. In general, Adams represented the manufacturing and commercial elements of the northeast; Clay the western group desiring Federal expenditure on internal improvements (these two groups later formed the Whig Party); Crawford represented the old southern Republicans; Jackson the new Republicans of the frontier and ordinary people everywhere, now calling themselves Democratic Republicans or just Democrats. As no candidate received a majority of the electoral vote, the contest was decided in the House of Representatives, where Clay threw his support to Adams, who received the votes of thirteen states, with Jackson receiving seven and Crawford four.

Attorney General—John McP. Berrien 1829–31; Roger B. Taney 1831–33; Benjamin F. Butler 1833–37.

Postmaster General—Wm. T. Barry 1829–35; Amos Kendall 1835–37.

Secretary of the Navy—John Branch 1829–31; Levi Woodbury 1831–34; Mahlon Dickerson 1834–37.

VOTE

1828	Electoral Vote
Andrew Jackson (Democrat)	178
John Quincy Adams (Whig)	83
1832 [1]	
Andrew Jackson (Democrat)	219
Henry Clay (Whig)	49

8 MARTIN VAN BUREN

Born: December 5, 1782, at Kinderhook, N. Y.

Died: July 24, 1862, at Kinderhook, N. Y. Buried: Kinderhook, N. Y.

Married: Hannah Hoes (1783–1819) in 1807.

Public Career: County Surrogate; U. S. Senator; State Senator; State Attorney-General; Governor of New York; Secretary of State; Minister to England; Vice-President.

Presidential Term: 1837–41.

Vice-President: Richard M. Johnson.

CABINET

Secretary of State—John Forsyth.

Secretary of the Treasury—Levi Woodbury.

Secretary of War—Joel R. Poinsett.

Attorney General—Benjamin F. Butler 1837–38; Felix Grundy 1838–40; Henry D. Gilpin 1840–41.

Postmaster General—Amos Kendall 1837–40; John M. Niles 1840–41.

Secretary of the Navy—Mahlon Dickerson 1837–38; James K. Paulding 1838–41.

[1] For this election, national conventions of parties were held to select nominees.

VOTE

1836	Popular Vote[1]	Electoral Vote
Martin Van Buren (Democrat)	762,978	170
Wm. Henry Harrison (Whig)	548,966	73

9 WILLIAM HENRY HARRISON

Born: February 9, 1773, at Berkeley, Va.
Died: April 4, 1841, at Washington, D. C. Buried: North Bend, Ohio.
Married: Anna Symmes (1775–1864) in 1795.
Public Career: Congressman; Governor, Territory of Indiana; Major-General; Member of Ohio Senate; U. S. Senator; Minister to Colombia.
Presidential Term: 1841.
Vice-President: John Tyler.

CABINET

Secretary of State—Daniel Webster.
Secretary of the Treasury—Thomas Ewing.
Secretary of War—John Bell.
Attorney General—John J. Crittenden.
Postmaster General—Francis Granger.
Secretary of the Navy—George E. Badger.

VOTE

1840	Popular Vote	Electoral Vote
Wm. Henry Harrison (Whig)	1,275,016	234
Martin Van Buren (Democrat)	1,129,102	60

[1] All states but South Carolina now chose electors by popular vote; though not complete until after the Civil War, popular votes are given henceforth.

10 JOHN TYLER

Born: March 29, 1790, at Greenway, Va.
Died: January 18, 1862, at Richmond, Va. Buried: Richmond, Va.
Married: Letitia Christian (1790–1842) in 1813, and Julia Gardiner (1820–1889) in 1844.
Public Career: Member of Virginia Legislature; Congressman; Governor of Virginia; U. S. Senator; Vice-President; Member of Confederate Congress.
Presidential Term: 1841–45.
Vice-President: None.

CABINET

Secretary of State–Daniel Webster 1841–43; Hugh S. Legaré 1843; Abel P. Upshur 1843–44; John C. Calhoun 1844–45.
Secretary of the Treasury–Thomas Ewing 1841; Walter Forward 1841–43; John C. Spencer 1843–44; George M. Bibb 1844–45.
Secretary of War–John Bell 1841; John C. Spencer 1841–43; James M. Porter 1843–44; William Wilkins 1844–45.
Attorney General–John J. Crittenden 1841; Hugh S. Legaré 1841–43; John Nelson 1843–45.
Postmaster General–Francis Granger 1841; Charles A. Wickliffe 1841–45.
Secretary of the Navy–George E. Badger 1841; Abel P. Upshur 1841–43; David Henshaw 1843–44; Thomas W. Gilmer 1844; John Y. Mason 1844–45.

11 JAMES K. POLK

Born: November 2, 1795, near Little Sugar Creek, N. C.
Died: June 15, 1849, at Nashville, Tenn. Buried: Nashville, Tenn.
Married: Sarah Childress (1803–1891) in 1824.
Public Career: Member of Tennessee Legislature; Member of Congress; Governor of Tennessee; Speaker of House of Representatives.

Presidential Term: 1845—49.
Vice-President: George M. Dallas.

CABINET

Secretary of State—James Buchanan.
Secretary of the Treasury—Robert J. Walker.
Secretary of War—William L. Marcy.
Attorney General—John Y. Mason 1845—46; Nathan Clifford
   1846—48; Isaac Toucey 1848—49.
Postmaster General—Cave Johnson.
Secretary of the Navy—George Bancroft 1845—46; John Y.
   Mason 1846—49.

VOTE

1844	Popular Vote	Electoral Vote
James K. Polk (Democrat)	1,337,243	170
Henry Clay (Whig)	1,299,068	105

12 ZACHARY TAYLOR

Born: November 24, 1784, in Orange County, Va.
Died: July 9, 1850, at Washington, D. C. Buried: near Louisville,
   Ky.
Married: Margaret Smith (1788—1852) in 1810.
Public Career: Major-General.
Presidential Term: 1849—50.
Vice-President: Millard Fillmore.

CABINET

Secretary of State—John M. Clayton.
Secretary of the Treasury—Wm. M. Meredith.
Secretary of War—George W. Crawford.
Attorney General—Reverdy Johnson.
Postmaster General—Jacob Collamer.
Secretary of the Navy—Wm. B. Preston.
Secretary of the Interior—Thomas Ewing.

VOTE

	Popular Vote	Electoral Vote
1848		
Zachary Taylor (Whig)	1,360,101	163
Lewis Cass (Democrat)	1,220,544	127

13. MILLARD FILLMORE

Born: January 7, 1800, in Cayuga County, N. Y.
Died: March 8, 1874, at Buffalo, N. Y. Buried: Buffalo, N. Y.
Married: Abigail Powers (1798–1853) in 1826, and Caroline Carmichael McIntosh (1813–1881) in 1858.
Public Career: Member of New York Assembly; Member of Congress; Comptroller of New York State; Vice-President.
Presidential Term: 1850–53.
Vice-President: None.

CABINET

Secretary of State—Daniel Webster 1850–52; Edward Everett 1852–53.
Secretary of the Treasury—Thomas Corwin.
Secretary of War—Charles M. Conrad.
Attorney General—John J. Crittenden.
Postmaster General—Nathan K. Hall 1850–52; Samuel D. Hubbard 1852–53.
Secretary of the Navy—Wm. A. Graham 1850–52; John P. Kennedy 1852–53.
Secretary of the Interior—T. M. T. McKennan 1850; Alex H. H. Stuart 1850–53.

14 FRANKLIN PIERCE

Born: November 23, 1804, at Hillsboro, N. H.
Died: October 8, 1869, at Concord, N. H. Buried: Concord, N. H.

Married: Jane Appleton (1806–1863) in 1834.
Public Career: Member of New Hampshire Legislature; U. S. Senator; Brigadier-General; Congressman.
Presidential Term: 1853–57.
Vice-President: William R. King 1853.

CABINET

Secretary of State—William L. Marcy.
Secretary of the Treasury—James Guthrie.
Secretary of War—Jefferson Davis.
Attorney General—Caleb Cushing.
Postmaster General—James Campbell.
Secretary of the Navy—James C. Dobbin.
Secretary of the Interior—Robert McClelland.

VOTE

1852	Popular Vote	Electoral Vote
Franklin Pierce (Democrat)	1,601,474	254
Winfield Scott (Whig)	1,386,578	42

15 JAMES BUCHANAN

Born: April 23, 1791, near Mercersburg, Pa.
Died: June 1, 1868, at Lancaster, Pa. Buried: Wheatland, Pa.
Unmarried.
Public Career: Member of Pennsylvania Legislature; Member of Congress; Minister to Russia; U. S. Senator (thrice); Secretary of State; Minister to England.
Presidential Term: 1857–61.
Vice-President: John C. Breckinridge.

CABINET

Secretary of State—Lewis Cass 1857–60; Jeremiah S. Black 1860–61.
Secretary of the Treasury—Howell Cobb 1857–60; Philip F. Thomas 1860–61; John A. Dix 1861.

Secretary of War—John B. Floyd 1857—61; Joseph Holt 1861.
Attorney General—Jeremiah S. Black 1857—60; Edwin M. Stanton
1860—61.
Postmaster General—Aaron V. Brown 1857—59; Joseph Holt
1859—61; Horatio King 1861.
Secretary of the Navy—Isaac Toucey.
Secretary of the Interior—Jacob Thompson.

VOTE

1856	*Popular Vote*	*Electoral Vote*
James Buchanan (Democrat)	1,927,995	174
John Frémont (Republican[1])	1,391,555	114
Millard Fillmore (Whig[1])	874,534	8

16 ABRAHAM LINCOLN

Born: February 12, 1809, in Hardin County, Ky.
Died: April 15, 1865, at Washington, D. C. Buried: Springfield,
Ill.
Married: Mary Todd (1818—1882) in 1842.
Public Career: Member of Illinois Legislature; Member of Congress.
Presidential Terms: 1861—65.
Vice-Presidents: Hannibal Hamlin 1861—65; Andrew Johnson
1865.

CABINET

Secretary of State—Wm. H. Seward.
Secretary of the Treasury—Salmon P. Chase 1861—64; Wm. P.
Fessenden 1864—65; Hugh McCulloch 1865.
Secretary of War—Simon Cameron 1861—62; Edwin M. Stanton
1862—65.
Attorney General—Edward Bates 1861—64; James Speed 1864—65.

[1] The Republican Party was founded by parts of the old Whig Party, dissident northern Democrats, and others. Some Whigs tried to keep their party alive, nominating Fillmore.

Postmaster General—Montgomery Blair 1861–64; William Dennison 1864–65.
Secretary of the Navy—Gideon Welles.
Secretary of the Interior—Caleb B. Smith 1861–63; John P. Usher 1863–65.

VOTE

1860	Popular Vote	Electoral Vote
Abraham Lincoln (Republican)	1,866,352	180
Stephen A. Douglas (Democrat— northern group[1])	1,375,157	12
John C. Breckenridge (Democrat— southern group[1])	849,781	72
John Bell (Constitutional Union, formerly Whig)	588,897	39
1864[2]		
Abraham Lincoln (Republican)	2,216,067	212
George B. McClellan (Democrat)	1,808,725	21

17 ANDREW JOHNSON

Born: December 29, 1808, at Raleigh, N. C.
Died: July 31, 1875, near Carter's Depot, Tenn. Buried: Greenville, Tenn.
Married: Eliza McCardle (1810–1876) in 1827.
Public Career: City Alderman; Mayor; Member of Tennessee Legislature; State Senator; Congressman; Governor of Tennessee; U. S. Senator; Military Governor of Tennessee; Vice-President.
Presidential Term: 1865–69.
Vice-President: None.

CABINET

Secretary of State—William H. Seward.
Secretary of the Treasury—Hugh McCulloch.

[1] The Democratic Party split over the slave issue, each group nominating for President.
[2] Southern states that had seceded did not vote in this election.

Secretary of War—Edwin M. Stanton 1865–67; U. S. Grant (*acting*) 1867–68; John M. Schofield 1868–69.
Attorney General—James Speed 1865–66; Henry Stanbery 1866–68; Wm. M. Evarts 1868–69.
Postmaster General—Wm. Dennison 1865–66; Alex. W. Randall 1866–69.
Secretary of the Navy—Gideon Welles.
Secretary of the Interior—John P. Usher 1865; James Harlan 1865–66; Orv. H. Browning 1866–69.

18   ULYSSES SIMPSON GRANT

Born: April 27, 1822, at Point Pleasant, Ohio.
Died: July 23, 1885; at Mt. McGregor, N. Y. Buried: New York City.
Married: Julia Dent (1826–1902) in 1848.
Public Career: Soldier and General.
Presidential Terms: 1869–77.
Vice-President: Schuyler Colfax 1869–73; Henry Wilson 1873–75.

CABINET

Secretary of State—Elihu B. Washburne 1869; Hamilton Fish 1869–77.
Secretary of the Treasury—George S. Boutwell 1869–73; Wm. A. Richardson 1873–74; Benjamin H. Bristow 1874–76; Lot M. Morrill 1876–77.
Secretary of War—John A. Rawlins 1869; Wm. T. Sherman 1869; Wm. W. Belknap 1869–76; Alphonso Taft 1876; James D. Cameron 1876–77.
Attorney General—Ebenezer R. Hoar 1869–70; Amos T. Akerman 1870–71; George H. Williams 1871–74; Edwards Pierrepont 1875–76; Alphonso Taft 1876–77.
Postmaster General—John A. J. Creswell 1869–74; James W. Marshall 1874; Marshall Jewell 1874–76; James N. Tyner 1876–77.
Secretary of the Navy—Adolph E. Borie 1869; George M. Robeson 1869–77.

Secretary of the Interior—Jacob D. Cox 1869–70; Columbus Delano 1870–75; Zachariah Chandler 1875–77.

VOTE

1868	Popular Vote	Electoral Vote
U. S. Grant (Republican)	3,015,071	214
Horatio Seymour (Democrat)	2,709,615	80
1872		
U. S. Grant (Republican)	3,597,132	286
Horace Greeley (Dem-Liberal)[1]	2,834,125	
Thos. A. Hendricks (Democrat)		42

19 RUTHERFORD BIRCHARD HAYES

Born: October 4, 1822, at Delaware, Ohio.
Died: January 17, 1893, at Fremont, Ohio. Buried: Fremont, Ohio.
Married: Lucy Webb (1831–1889) in 1852.
Public Career: City Attorney; Brigadier-General; Congressman; Governor of Ohio.
Presidential Term: 1877–81.
Vice-President: Wm. A. Wheeler.

CABINET

Secretary of State—Wm. M. Evarts.
Secretary of the Treasury—John Sherman.
Secretary of War—George W. McCrary 1877–79; Alexander Ramsey 1879–81.
Attorney General—Charles Devens.
Postmaster General—David McK. Key 1877–80; Horace Maynard 1880–81.
Secretary of the Navy—Richard W. Thompson 1877–81; Nathan Goff, Jr. 1881.
Secretary of the Interior—Carl Schurz.

[1] Greeley died between the time of election and counting of electoral votes, so his electoral votes were cast for Hendricks, a leading Democrat.

VOTE

	Popular Vote	Electoral Vote
1876[1]		
Rutherford B. Hayes (Republican)	4,033,950	185
Samuel J. Tilden (Democrat)	4,285,992	184

20 JAMES ABRAM GARFIELD

Born: November 19, 1831, at Orange, Ohio.
Died: September 19, 1881, at Elberon, N. J. Buried: Cleveland, Ohio.
Married: Lucretia Rudolph (1832–1918) in 1858.
Public Career: Ohio State Senator; Major-General; Congressman; Senator-elect.
Presidential Term: 1881.
Vice-President: Chester A. Arthur.

CABINET

Secretary of State—James G. Blaine.
Secretary of the Treasury—Wm. Windom.
Secretary of War—Robert T. Lincoln.
Attorney General—Wayne MacVeagh.
Postmaster General—Thomas L. James.
Secretary of the Navy—Wm. H. Hunt.
Secretary of the Interior—Sam J. Kirkwood.

VOTE

	Popular Vote	Electoral Vote
1880		
James A. Garfield (Republican)	4,449,053	214
Winfield S. Hancock (Democrat)	4,442,030	155

[1] The election was contested, so Congress appointed an Electoral Commission to investigate. The commission, by a strict party vote, awarded the twenty-two electoral votes of Florida, Louisiana, Oregon, and South Carolina to the Republican candidate, whereupon Congress declared Hayes elected.

21 CHESTER ALAN ARTHUR

Born: October 5, 1830, at Fairfield, Vt.
Died: November 18, 1886, at New York City. Buried: Albany, N. Y.
Married: Ellen Herndon (1837–1880) in 1859.
Public Career: Quartermaster General of New York State; Collector of Port of New York; Vice-President.
Presidential Term: 1881–85.
Vice-President: None.

CABINET

Secretary of State—James G. Blaine 1881; F. T. Frelinghuysen 1881–85.
Secretary of the Treasury—Wm. Windom 1881; Chas. J. Folger 1881–84; Walter Q. Gresham 1884; Hugh McCulloch 1884–85.
Secretary of War—Robert T. Lincoln.
Attorney General—Wayne MacVeagh 1881; Benj. H. Brewster 1881–85.
Postmaster General—Thomas L. James 1881; Timothy O. Howe 1881–83; Walter Q. Gresham 1883–84; Frank Hatton 1884–85.
Secretary of the Navy—Wm. H. Hunt 1881–82; Wm. E. Chandler 1882–85.
Secretary of the Interior—Sam J. Kirkwood 1881–82; Henry M. Teller 1882–85.

22 and 24 GROVER CLEVELAND

Born: March 18, 1837, at Caldwell, N. J.
Died: June 24, 1908, at Princeton, N. J. Buried: Princeton, N. J.
Married: Frances Folsom (1864–1947) in 1886.
Public Career: Asst. District Attorney and Sheriff of Erie County; Mayor of Buffalo; Governor of New York.
Presidential Terms: 1885–89 and 1893–97.
Vice-Presidents: Thos. A. Hendricks 1885; Adlai E. Stevenson 1893–97.

CABINET

Secretary of State—Thomas F. Bayard 1885–89; Walter Q. Gresham 1893–95; Richard Olney 1895–97.
Secretary of the Treasury—Daniel Manning 1885–87; Charles S. Fairchild 1887–89; John G. Carlisle 1893–97.
Secretary of War—Wm. C. Endicott 1885–89; Daniel S. Lamont 1893–97.
Attorney General—Augustus H. Garland 1885–89; Richard Olney 1893–95; Judson Harmon 1895–97.
Postmaster General—Wm. F. Vilas 1885–88; Don M. Dickinson 1888–89; Wilson S. Bissel 1893–95; William L. Wilson 1895–97.
Secretary of the Navy—Wm. C. Whitney 1885–89; Hilary A. Herbert 1893–97.
Secretary of the Interior—Lucius Q. C. Lamar 1885–88; Wm. F. Vilas 1888–89; Hoke Smith 1893–96; David R. Francis 1896–97.
Secretary of Agriculture—Norman J. Colman 1889; J. Sterling Morton 1893–97.

VOTE

1884	Popular Vote	Electoral Vote
Grover Cleveland (Democrat)	4,911,017	219
James G. Blaine (Republican)	4,848,334	182
1892		
Grover Cleveland (Democrat)	5,554,414	277
Benj. Harrison (Republican)	5,190,802	145
James B. Weaver (Peoples)	1,027,329	22

23 BENJAMIN HARRISON

Born: August 20, 1833, at North Bend, Ohio.
Died: March 13, 1901, at Indianapolis, Ind. Buried: Indianapolis, Ind.
Married: Caroline Scott (1832–92) in 1853, and Mary Lord Dimmick (1858–1948) in 1896.
Public Career: Reporter in Supreme Court of Indiana; Brigadier-General; U. S. Senator.

Presidential Term: 1889–93.
Vice-President: Levi P. Morton.

CABINET

Secretary of State—James G. Blaine 1889–92; John W. Foster
1892–93.
Secretary of the Treasury—Wm. Windom 1889–91; Charles
Foster 1891–93.
Secretary of War—Redfield Proctor 1889–91; Stephen B. Elkins
1891–93.
Attorney General—Wm. H. H. Miller.
Postmaster General—John Wanamaker.
Secretary of the Navy—Benjamin F. Tracy.
Secretary of the Interior—John W. Noble.
Secretary of Agriculture—Jeremiah M. Rusk.

VOTE

1888	Popular Vote	Electoral Vote
Benjamin Harrison (Republican)	5,444,337	233
Grover Cleveland (Democrat)	5,540,050	168

25 WILLIAM McKINLEY

Born: January 29, 1843, at Niles, Ohio.
Died: September 14, 1901, at Buffalo, N. Y. Buried: Canton,
Ohio.
Married: Ida Saxton (1847–1907) in 1871.
Public Career: Major; County Attorney; Member of Congress;
Governor of Ohio.
Presidential Term: 1897–1901.
Vice-Presidents: Garret A. Hobart 1897–99; Theodore Roose-
velt 1901.

CABINET

Secretary of State—John Sherman 1897–98; Wm. R. Day 1898;
John Hay 1898–1901.
Secretary of the Treasury—Lyman J. Gage.

Secretary of War–Russell A. Alger 1897–99; Elihu Root 1899–1901.
Attorney General–Joseph McKenna 1897–98; John W. Griggs 1898–1901; Philander C. Knox 1901.
Postmaster General–James A. Gary 1897–98; Charles Emory Smith 1898–1901.
Secretary of the Navy–John D. Long.
Secretary of the Interior–Cornelius N. Bliss 1897–98; Ethan A. Hitchcock 1898–1901.
Secretary of Agriculture–James Wilson.

VOTE

1896	Popular Vote	Electoral Vote
William McKinley (Republican)	7,035,638	271
Wm. J. Bryan (Democrat-Peoples)	6,467,946	176
1900		
William McKinley (Republican)	7,219,530	292
Wm. J. Bryan (Democrat-Peoples)	6,358,071	155

26 THEODORE ROOSEVELT

Born: October 27, 1858, at New York City.
Died: January 6, 1919, at Oyster Bay, N. Y. Buried: Oyster Bay, N. Y.
Married: Alice Lee (1861–84) in 1880 and Edith Kermit Carow (1861–1948) in 1886.
Public Career: Member of New York Legislature; United States Civil Service Commissioner; New York Police Commissioner; Assistant Secretary of Navy; Colonel; Governor of New York; Vice-President.
Presidential Terms: 1901–09.
Vice-President: Chas. W. Fairbanks 1905–09.

CABINET

Secretary of State–John Hay 1901–05; Elihu Root 1905–09; Robert Bacon 1909.
Secretary of the Treasury–Lyman J. Gage 1901–02; Leslie M. Shaw 1902–07; George B. Cortelyou 1907–09.

Secretary of War–Elihu Root 1901–04; Wm. H. Taft 1904–08; Luke E. Wright 1908–09.

Attorney General–Philander C. Knox 1901–04; Wm. H. Moody 1904–06; Chas. J. Bonaparte 1906–09.

Postmaster General–Chas. Emory Smith 1901–02; Henry C. Payne 1902–04; Robert J. Wynne 1904–05; George B. Cortelyou 1905–07; George von L. Meyer 1907–09.

Secretary of the Navy–John D. Long 1901–02; Wm. H. Moody 1902–04; Paul Morton 1904–05; Chas. J. Bonaparte 1905–06; Victor H. Metcalf 1906–08; Truman H. Newberry 1908–09.

Secretary of the Interior–Ethan A. Hitchcock 1901–07; James R. Garfield 1907–09.

Secretary of Agriculture–James Wilson.

Secretary of Commerce & Labor–Geo. B. Cortelyou 1903–04; Victor H. Metcalf 1904–06; Oscar S. Straus 1906–09.

VOTE

1904	Popular Vote	Electoral Vote
Theodore Roosevelt (Republican)	7,628,834	336
Alton B. Parker (Democrat)	5,084,491	140

27 WILLIAM HOWARD TAFT

Born: September 15, 1857, at Cincinnati, Ohio.

Died: March 8, 1930, at Washington, D. C. Buried: Arlington National Cemetery, Arlington County, Va.

Married: Helen Herron (1861–1943) in 1886.

Public Career: Assistant Prosecuting Attorney; Collector of Internal Revenue; Solicitor General of U. S.; U. S. Circuit Judge; Governor of Philippines; Secretary of War; Chief Justice of U. S. Supreme Court.

Presidential Term: 1909–13.

Vice-President: James S. Sherman 1909–12.

CABINET

Secretary of State–Philander C. Knox.

Secretary of the Treasury—Franklin MacVeagh.
Secretary of War—Jacob M. Dickinson 1909—11; Henry L. Stimson 1911—13.
Attorney General—George W. Wickersham.
Postmaster General—F. H. Hitchcock.
Secretary of the Navy—George von L. Meyer.
Secretary of the Interior—Richard A. Ballinger 1909—11; Walter L. Fisher 1911—13.
Secretary of Agriculture—James Wilson.
Secretary of Commerce & Labor—Charles Nagel.

VOTE

1908	Popular Vote	Electoral Vote
Wm. Howard Taft (Republican)	7,679,006	321
Wm. J. Bryan (Democrat)	6,409,106	162

28 WOODROW WILSON

Born: December 28, 1856, at Staunton, Va.
Died: February 3, 1924, at Washington, D. C. Buried: Washington, D. C.
Married: Ellen Axson (1860—1914) in 1885, and Edith Bolling Galt (1872—1961) in 1915.
Public Career: Governor of New Jersey.
Presidential Terms: 1913—21.
Vice-President: Thomas R. Marshall.

CABINET

Secretary of State—William J. Bryan 1913—15; Robert Lansing 1915—20; Bainbridge Colby 1920—21.
Secretary of the Treasury—William G. McAdoo 1913—18; Carter Glass 1918—20; David F. Houston 1920—21.
Secretary of War—Lindley M. Garrison 1913—16; Newton D. Baker 1916—21.
Attorney General—J. C. McReynolds 1913—14; Thomas W. Gregory 1914—19; A. M. Palmer 1919—21.
Postmaster General—Albert S. Burleson.

Secretary of the Navy—Josephus Daniels.
Secretary of the Interior—Franklin K. Lane 1913–20; John B. Payne 1920–21.
Secretary of Agriculture—David F. Houston 1913–20; Edw. T. Meredith 1920–21.
Secretary of Commerce—Wm. C. Redfield 1913–19; Josh. W. Alexander 1919–21.
Secretary of Labor—William B. Wilson.

VOTE

1912	Popular Vote	Electoral Vote
Woodrow Wilson (Democrat)	6,286,214	435
Theodore Roosevelt (Progressive)[1]	4,216,020	88
Wm. Howard Taft (Republican)	3,483,922	8
1916		
Woodrow Wilson (Democrat)	9,129,606	277
Charles E. Hughes (Republican)	8,538,221	254

29 WARREN GAMALIEL HARDING

Born: November 2, 1865, at Corsica, Ohio.
Died: August 2, 1923, at San Francisco, Calif. Buried: Marion, Ohio.
Married: Florence Kling DeWolfe (1860–1924) in 1891.
Public Career: Member of Ohio State Senate; Lieutenant-Governor of Ohio; U. S. Senator.
Presidential Term: 1921–23.
Vice-President: Calvin Coolidge.

CABINET

Secretary of State—Charles E. Hughes.
Secretary of the Treasury—Andrew W. Mellon.
Secretary of War—John W. Weeks.
Attorney General—H. M. Daugherty.
Postmaster General—Will H. Hays 1921–22; Hubert Work 1922–23; Harry S. New 1923.

[1] The Progressive Party was chiefly a split from the Republican Party.

Secretary of the Navy—Edwin Denby.
Secretary of the Interior—Albert B. Fall 1921–23; Hubert Work
1923.
Secretary of Agriculture—Henry C. Wallace.
Secretary of Commerce—Herbert C. Hoover.
Secretary of Labor—James J. Davis.

VOTE

1920	Popular Vote	Electoral Vote
Warren G. Harding (Republican)	16,152,200	404
James M. Cox (Democrat)	9,147,353	127

30 CALVIN COOLIDGE

Born: July 4, 1872, at Plymouth, Vt.
Died: January 5, 1933, at Northampton, Mass. Buried: Plymouth,
Vt.
Married: Grace Goodhue (1879–1957) in 1905.
Public Career: Member of City Council at Northampton; City
Solicitor; Clerk of Courts; Member of Massachusetts Legisla-
ture; Mayor of Northampton; State Senator; Lieutenant-Gover-
nor of Massachusetts; Governor of Massachusetts; Vice-Presi-
dent.
Presidential Terms: 1923–29.
Vice-President: Charles G. Dawes 1925–29.

CABINET

Secretary of State—Charles E. Hughes 1923–25; Frank B. Kellogg
1925–29.
Secretary of the Treasury—Andrew W. Mellon.
Secretary of War—John W. Weeks 1923–25; Dwight F. Davis
1925–29.
Attorney General—H. M. Daugherty 1923–24; Harlan F. Stone
1924–25; John G. Sargent 1925–29.
Postmaster General—Harry S. New.
Secretary of the Navy—Edwin Denby 1923–24; Curtis D. Wilbur
1924–29.

Secretary of the Interior—Hubert Work 1923–28; Roy O. West 1928–29.
Secretary of Agriculture—Henry C. Wallace 1923–24; Howard M. Gore 1924–25; W. M. Jardine 1925–29.
Secretary of Commerce—Herbert C. Hoover 1923–28; Wm. F. Whiting 1928–29.
Secretary of Labor—James J. Davis.

VOTE

1924	Popular Vote	Electoral Vote
Calvin Coolidge (Republican)	15,725,016	382
John W. Davis (Democrat)	8,385,586	136
Robert M. La Folette (Progressive)[1]	4,822,856	13

31　HERBERT CLARK HOOVER

Born: August 10, 1874, at West Branch, Iowa.
Died: October 20, 1964, at New York City, N.Y. Buried: West Branch, Iowa.
Married: Lou Henry (1875–1944) in 1899.
Public Career: Chairman of American Relief Committee; Chairman of Commission for the Relief of Belgium; U. S. Food Administrator; Secretary of Commerce.
Presidential Term: 1929–33.
Vice-President: Charles Curtis.

CABINET

Secretary of State—Henry L. Stimson.
Secretary of the Treasury—Andrew W. Mellon 1929–32; Ogden L. Mills 1932–33.
Secretary of War—James W. Good 1929; Patrick J. Hurley 1929–33.
Attorney General—Wm. D. Mitchell.
Postmaster General—Walter F. Brown.
Secretary of the Navy—Charles Francis Adams.
Secretary of the Interior—Ray Lyman Wilbur.
Secretary of Agriculture—Arthur M. Hyde.

[1] Not the same as the Roosevelt Progressive Party in 1912, but containing many of the same elements.

Secretary of Commerce—Robert P. Lamont 1929–32; Roy D. Chapin 1932–33.

Secretary of Labor—James J. Davis 1929–30; Wm. N. Doak 1930–33.

VOTE

1928	Popular Vote	Electoral Vote
Herbert C. Hoover (Republican)	21,392,190	444
Alfred E. Smith (Democrat)	15,016,443	87

32 FRANKLIN DELANO ROOSEVELT

Born: January 30, 1882, at Hyde Park, N. Y.
Died: April 12, 1945, at Warm Springs, Ga. Buried: Hyde Park, N. Y.
Married: Anna Eleanor Roosevelt (1884–1962) in 1905.
Public Career: New York State Senator; Assistant Secretary of the Navy; Governor of New York.
Presidential Terms: 1933–45.
Vice-Presidents: John Nance Garner 1933–41; Henry Agard Wallace 1941–45; Harry S. Truman 1945.

CABINET

Secretary of State—Cordell Hull 1933–44; E. R. Stettinius, Jr. 1944–45.
Secretary of the Treasury—Wm. H. Woodin 1933–34; Henry Morgenthau, Jr. 1934–45.
Secretary of War—George H. Dern 1933–36; Harry H. Woodring 1936–40; Henry L. Stimson 1940–45.
Attorney General—Homer S. Cummings 1933–39; Frank Murphy 1939–40; Robert H. Jackson 1940–41; Francis Biddle 1941–45.
Postmaster General—James A. Farley 1933–40; Frank C. Walker 1940–45.
Secretary of the Navy—Claude A. Swanson 1933–40; Charles Edison 1940; Frank Knox 1940–44; James V. Forrestal 1944–45.
Secretary of the Interior—Harold L. Ickes.

Secretary of Agriculture—Henry A. Wallace 1933–40; Claude R. Wickard 1940–45.
Secretary of Commerce—Daniel C. Roper 1933–39; Harry L. Hopkins 1939–40; Jesse Jones 1940–45; Henry A. Wallace 1945.
Secretary of Labor—Frances Perkins.

VOTE

	Popular Vote	Electoral Vote
1932		
Franklin D. Roosevelt (Democrat)	22,821,857	472
Herbert Hoover (Republican)	15,761,841	59
1936		
Franklin D. Roosevelt (Democrat)	27,476,673	523
Alf M. Landon (Republican)	16,679,583	8
1940		
Franklin D. Roosevelt (Democrat)	27,243,466	449
Wendell Willkie (Republican)	22,304,755	82
1944		
Franklin D. Roosevelt (Democrat)	25,602,505	432
Thomas E. Dewey (Republican)	22,006,278	99

33 HARRY S. TRUMAN

Born: May 8, 1884, at Lamar, Mo.
Died: December 26, 1972, at Kansas City, Mo. Buried: Independence, Mo.
Married: Bess Wallace (1885–1982) in 1919.
Public Career: Army Captain; County Judge; U. S. Senator; Vice-President.
Presidential Terms: 1945–53.
Vice-President: Alben W. Barkley 1949–53.

CABINET

Secretary of State—Edward R. Stettinius, Jr. 1945; James F. Byrnes 1945–47; George C. Marshall 1947–49; Dean G. Acheson 1949–53.
Secretary of the Treasury—Henry Morgenthau, Jr. 1945; Fred M. Vinson 1945–46; John W. Snyder 1946–53.
Secretary of War—Henry L. Stimson 1945; Robert P. Patterson

1945—47; Kenneth C. Royall 1947. (The Secretary of War ceased to be a member of the President's Cabinet on the creation of the Department of Defense in 1947.)

Secretary of the Navy—James Forrestal 1945—47. (The Secretary of the Navy ceased to be a member of the President's Cabinet on the creation of the Department of Defense in 1947.)

Secretary of Defense (position created in 1947)—James Forrestal 1947—49; Louis A. Johnson 1949—50; George C. Marshall 1950—51; Robert A. Lovett 1951—53.

Attorney General—Francis Biddle 1945; Thomas C. Clark 1945—49; James H. McGrath 1949—52; James P. McGranery 1952—53.

Postmaster General—Frank C. Walker 1945; Robert E. Hannegan 1945—47; Jesse M. Donaldson 1947—53.

Secretary of the Interior—Harold Ickes 1945—46; Julius A. Krug 1946—49; Oscar L. Chapman 1949—53.

Secretary of Agriculture—Claude R. Wickard 1945; Clinton P. Anderson 1945—48; Charles F. Brannan 1948—53.

Secretary of Commerce—Henry A. Wallace 1945—46; Averell Harriman 1946—48; Charles Sawyer 1948—53.

Secretary of Labor—Frances Perkins 1945; Lewis B. Schwellenbach 1945—48; Maurice J. Tobin 1948—53.

VOTE

1948	Popular Vote	Electoral Vote
Harry S. Truman (Democrat)	24,105,695	303
Thomas E. Dewey (Republican)	21,969,170	189
J. Strom Thurmond (States' Rights Democrat)	1,169,021	39
Henry A. Wallace (Progressive)	1,156,103	0

34 DWIGHT D. EISENHOWER

Born: October 14, 1890, in Denison, Tex.

Died: March 28, 1969, at Washington, D.C. Buried: Abilene, Kansas.

Married: Mamie Geneva Doud (1896—1979) in 1916.

Public Career: Rose to rank of General of the Army; Commanding General, Allied Forces, European Theatre of Operations,

World War II; Supreme Commander, Integrated European Defense Force, 1950.
Presidential Terms: 1953–61.
Vice-President: Richard M. Nixon.

CABINET

Secretary of State—John F. Dulles 1953–59; Christian A. Herter 1959–61.
Secretary of the Treasury—George M. Humphrey 1953–57; Robert B. Anderson 1957–61.
Secretary of Defense—Charles E. Wilson 1953–57; Neil H. McElroy 1957–59; Thomas S. Gates, Jr. 1959–61.
Attorney General—Herbert Brownell, Jr. 1953–57; William P. Rogers 1957–61.
Postmaster General—Arthur E. Summerfield.
Secretary of the Interior—Douglas McKay 1953–56; Frederick A. Seaton 1956–61.
Secretary of Agriculture—Ezra T. Benson.
Secretary of Commerce—Sinclair Weeks 1953–59; Frederick H. Mueller 1959–61.
Secretary of Labor—Martin P. Durkin 1953; James P. Mitchell 1953–61.
Secretary of Health, Education, and Welfare (position created in 1953)—Oveta C. Hobby 1953–55; Marion B. Folsom 1955–58; Arthur S. Flemming 1958–61.

VOTE

1952	Popular Vote	Electoral Vote
Dwight D. Eisenhower (Republican)	33,927,549	442
Adlai E. Stevenson (Democrat)	27,311,316	89
1956		
Dwight D. Eisenhower (Republican)	35,575,420	457
Adlai E. Stevenson (Democrat)	26,033,066	73

35 JOHN F. KENNEDY

Born: May 29, 1917, in Brookline, Mass.
Died: Nov. 22, 1963, at Dallas, Tex. Buried: Arlington National
Cemetery, Arlington County, Va.
Married: Jacqueline Lee Bouvier (1929–   ) in 1953.
Public Career: Lieutenant, U. S. Navy; Congressman; U. S.
Senator.
Presidential Term: 1961–63.
Vice-President: Lyndon B. Johnson.

CABINET

Secretary of State—Dean Rusk 1961–63.
Secretary of the Treasury—Clarence D. Dillon 1961–63.
Secretary of Defense—Robert S. McNamara 1961–63.
Attorney General—Robert F. Kennedy 1961–63.
Postmaster General—J. Edward Day 1961–63; John A Gronou-
ski, 1963.
Secretary of the Interior—Stewart L. Udall 1961–63.
Secretary of Agriculture—Orville L. Freeman 1961–63.
Secretary of Commerce—Luther H. Hodges 1961–63.
Secretary of Labor—Arthur Goldberg 1961–62; W. Willard
Wirtz 1962–63.
Secretary of Health, Education, and Welfare—Abraham A. Ribi-
coff 1961–62; Anthony J. Celebrezze 1962–63.

VOTE

1960	Popular Vote	Electoral Vote
John F. Kennedy (Democrat)	34,221,463	303
Richard M. Nixon (Republican)	34,108,582	219

36 LYNDON B. JOHNSON

Born: Aug. 27, 1908, near Stonewall, Tex.
Died: January 22, 1973, on way to San Antonio, Tex. Buried:
Stonewall, Tex.
Married: Claudia Taylor (1912–   ) in 1934.
Public Career: Public school teacher; Administrator for Texas,
National Youth Administration; Congressman; Commander,

U. S. Naval Reserve; U.S. Senator; Vice-President.
Presidential Terms: 1963-69.
Vice-President: Hubert H. Humphrey, Jr. 1965–69.

CABINET

Secretary of State—Dean Rusk 1963–69.
Secretary of the Treasury—Clarence D. Dillon 1963–65; Henry
H. Fowler 1965–68; Joseph W. Barr 1968–69.
Secretary of Defense—Robert S. McNamara 1963–68; Clark M.
Clifford 1968–69.
Attorney General—Robert F. Kennedy 1963–64; Nicholas deB.
Katzenbach 1965–66; William R. Clark 1967–69.
Postmaster General—John A. Gronouski 1963–65; Lawrence F.
O'Brien 1965–68; W. Marvin Watson 1968–69.
Secretary of the Interior—Stewart L. Udall 1963–69.
Secretary of Agriculture—Orville L. Freeman, 1963–69.
Secretary of Commerce—Luther H. Hodges 1963–65; John T.
Connor 1965–67; Alexander B. Trowbridge 1967–68; Cyrus
R. Smith 1968–69.
Secretary of Labor—W. Willard Wirtz 1963–69.
Secretary of Health, Education, and Welfare—Anthony J. Cele-
brezze 1963–65; John W. Gardner 1965–68; Wilbur J. Cohen
1968–69; Robert C. Wood 1969.
Secretary of Housing and Urban Development (position created
in 1966)—Robert C. Weaver 1966–69.
Secretary of Transportation (position created in 1967)—Alan S.
Boyd 1967–69.

VOTE

1964	Popular Vote	Electoral Vote
Lyndon B. Johnson (Democrat)	43,121,085	486
Barry M. Goldwater (Republican)	27,145,161	52

37 RICHARD M. NIXON

Born: Jan. 9, 1913, in Yorba Linda, Calif.
Married: Patricia Ryan (1912–   ) in 1940.
Public Career: Lt. Commander, U.S. Navy; Congressman; U.S.
Senator; Vice-President.
Presidential Terms: 1969–74.

Vice President: Spiro T. Agnew 1969–73; Gerald R. Ford 1973–74.

CABINET [1]

Secretary of State—William P. Rogers 1969–73; Henry Kissinger 1973-74.
Secretary of the Treasury—David M. Kennedy 1969–71; John B. Connally, Jr. 1971–72; George P. Schultz 1972–74; William E. Simon 1974.
Secretary of Defense—Melvin R. Laird 1969–73; Elliot L. Richardson 1973; James R. Schlesinger 1973–74.
Attorney General—John N. Mitchell 1969–72; Richard G. Kleindienst 1972–73; Elliot L. Richardson 1973; William B. Saxbe 1974.
Postmaster General—Winton M. Blount 1969–70[2].
Secretary of the Interior—Walter J. Hickel 1969–70; Rogers C. B. Morton 1971–74.
Secretary of Agriculture—Clifford M. Hardin 1969–71; Earl L. Butz 1971–74.
Secretary of Commerce—Maurice H. Stans 1969–72; Peter G. Peterson 1972–73; Frederick B. Dent 1973–74.
Secretary of Labor—George P. Schultz 1969–70; James D. Hodgson 1970–73; Peter J. Brennan 1973–74.
Secretary of Health, Education and Welfare—Robert H. Finch 1969–70; Elliot L. Richardson 1970–73; Caspar W. Weinberger 1973–74.
Secretary of Housing and Urban Development—George Romney 1969–73; James T. Lynn 1973–74.
Secretary of Transportation—John A. Volpe 1969–73; Claude S. Brinegar 1973–74.

VOTE

1968	Popular Vote	Electoral Vote
Richard M. Nixon (Republican)	31,770,237	301
Hubert H. Humphrey, Jr. (Democrat)	31,270,533	191
George C. Wallace (American Independent Party)	9,897,141	46

[1] Omitted here are persons "of cabinet rank" who are not heads of departments.
[2] The Postmaster General ceased to be a cabinet member when the Post Office Department was replaced in 1970 by an independent agency, the U.S. Postal Service.

1972
Richard M. Nixon (Republican)   47,168,963   520
George S. McGovern (Democrat)   29,169,615   17
John Hospers (Libertarian)   2,691   1

38   GERALD R. FORD

Born: July 14, 1913, in Omaha, Neb.
Married: Elizabeth B. Warren (1918-   ) in 1948.
Public Career: Lt. Commander, U.S. Naval Reserve; Congressman; Vice-President.
Presidential Term: 1974-77.
Vice-President: Nelson A. Rockefeller 1974–77.

CABINET

Secretary of State—Henry A. Kissinger 1974–77.
Secretary of the Treasury—William E. Simon 1974–77.
Secretary of Defense—James R. Schlesinger 1974–75; Donald H. Rumsfeld 1975-77.
Attorney General—William B. Saxbe 1974–75; Edward H. Levi 1975–77.
Secretary of the Interior—Rogers C. B. Morton 1974–75; Stanley K. Hathaway 1975; Thomas S. Kleppe 1975-77.
Secretary of Agriculture—Earl L. Butz 1974–76.
Secretary of Commerce—Frederick B. Dent 1974–75; Rogers C. B. Morton 1975; Elliott L. Richardson 1976–77.
Secretary of Labor—Peter J. Brennan 1974–75; John T. Dunlop 1975–76; Willie J. Usery, Jr. 1976–77.
Secretary of Health, Education and Welfare—Caspar W. Weinberger 1974–75; Forrest D. Mathews 1975–77.
Secretary of Housing and Urban Development—James T. Lynn 1974–75; Carla A. Hills 1975–77.
Secretary of Transportation—Claude S. Brinegar 1974–75; William T. Coleman, Jr., 1975–77.

VOTE

Ford was nominated for Vice-President by Richard M. Nixon, then confirmed by a vote of 92 to 3 in the Senate and 387 to 35 in the House of Representatives, under the XXV Amendment to the Constitution. He became President following Nixon's resignation.

39 JAMES EARL CARTER

Born: Oct. 1, 1924, in Plains, Ga.
Married: Rosalynn Smith (1927–   ) in 1946.
Public Career: Lieutenant, U.S. Navy; member, Sumter County School Board; Member, Georgia Senate; Governor of Georgia.
Presidential Term: 1977–81.
Vice-President: Walter F. Mondale 1977–81.

CABINET

Secretary of State—Cyrus R. Vance 1977–80; Edmund S. Muskie 1980–81.
Secretary of the Treasury—W. Michael Blumenthal 1977–79; G. William Miller 1979–81.
Secretary of Defense—Harold Brown 1977–81.
Attorney General—Griffin Bell 1977–79; Benjamin R. Civiletti 1979–81.
Secretary of the Interior—Cecil D. Andrus 1977–81.
Secretary of Agriculture—Bob Bergland 1977–81.
Secretary of Commerce—Juanita Kreps 1977–79; Philip M. Klutznick 1980–81.
Secretary of Labor—Ray Marshall 1977–81.
Secretary of Health, Education and Welfare—Joseph Califano 1977–79; Patricia R. Harris 1979–80 (position eliminated in 1980 when the Department of Health, Education and Welfare was fully split into two new agencies—the Department of Education and the Department of Health and Human Services).
Secretary of Housing and Urban Development—Patricia R. Harris 1977–79; Moon Landrieu 1979–81.
Secretary of Transportation—Brock Adams 1977–79; Neil Goldschmidt 1979–81.
Secretary of Energy (position created in 1977)—James R. Schlesinger 1977–79; Charles W. Duncan, Jr. 1979–81.
Secretary of Education (position created in 1979)—Shirley M. Hufstedler 1979–81.
Secretary of Health and Human Services (term first officially used in 1980 when the Department of Health and Human Services was fully established)—Patricia R. Harris 1980–81.

VOTE

1976	Popular Vote	Electoral Vote
James E. Carter (Democrat)	40,827,394	297
Gerald R. Ford (Republican)	39,145,977	240
Ronald Reagan	0	1

40 RONALD WILSON REAGAN

Born: Feb. 6, 1911, in Tampico, Ill.
Married: Jane Wyman (1917–   ) in 1940, divorced 1948, and Nancy Davis (1923–   ) in 1952.
Public Career: Captain, U.S. Army Air Forces; Governor of California.
Presidential Terms: 1981–
Vice-President: George H. W. Bush 1981–

CABINET

Secretary of State—Alexander M. Haig, Jr. 1981–82; George P. Shultz 1982–89

Secretary of Treasury—Donald T. Regan 1981–85; James A. Baker III 1985–88; Nicholas F. Brady 1988–89

Secretary of Defense—Caspar W. Weinberger 1981–87; Frank C. Carlucci 1987–89

Attorney General—William F. Smith 1981–85; Edwin Meese III 1985–88; Richard Thornburgh 1988–89

Secretary of the Interior—James G. Watt 1981–83; William P. Clark 1983–85; Donald P. Hodel 1985–89

Secretary of Agriculture—John R. Block 1981–88; Richard E. Lyng 1988–89

Secretary of Commerce—Malcolm Baldrige 1981–87; C. William Verity, Jr. 1987–89

Secretary of Labor—Raymond J. Donovan 1981–85; William E. Brock 1985–87; Ann D. McLaughlin 1987–89

Secretary of Health and Human Services—Richard S. Schweiker 1981–83; Margaret M. Heckler 1983–85; Otis R. Bowen 1985–89

Secretary of Housing and Urban Development—Samuel R. Pierce, Jr. 1981—89
Secretary of Transportation—Andrew L. Lewis Jr. 1981–83; Elizabeth H. Dole 1983–87; James H. Burnley IV 1987-89
Secretary of Energy—James B. Edwards 1981–82; Donald P. Hodel 1982–85; John S. Herrington 1985–89
Secretary of Education—Terrel H. Bell 1981–85; William J. Bennett 1985–88; Lauro F. Cavazos 1988–89

VOTE

1980	Popular Vote	Electoral Vote
Ronald W. Reagan (Republican)	43,899,248	489
James E. Carter (Democrat)	35,481,435	49
John B. Anderson (Independent)	5,719,437	0
1984		
Ronald W. Reagan (Republican)	52,836,865	525
Walter F. Mondale (Democrat)	36,553,669	13

41 GEORGE HERBERT WALKER BUSH

Born: June 12, 1924, in Milton, Mass.
Married: Barbara Pierce (1925–   ) in 1945.
Public Career: Lieutenant, U.S. Navy; Member of Congress; U.S. Permanent Representative to the UN; Chief Liaison Officer, Beijing; Director, Central Intelligence Agency; Vice President.
Presidential Term: 1989–
Vice President: Dan Quayle 1989–

CABINET

Secretary of State—James A. Baker III 1989–
Secretary of Treasury—Nicholas F. Brady 1989–
Secretary of Defense—Richard B. Cheney, 1989–
Attorney General—Richard L. Thornburgh, 1989–
Secretary of the Interior—Manuel Lujan Jr., 1989–

Secretary of Agriculture — Clayton K. Yeutter, 1989–
Secretary of Commerce — Robert A. Mosbacher, 1989–
Secretary of Labor — Elizabeth Hanford Dole, 1989–
Secretary of Health and Human Services — Dr. Louis W. Sullivan, 1989–
Secretary of Housing and Urban Development — Jack F. Kemp, 1989–
Secretary of Transportation — Samuel K. Skinner, 1989–
Secretary of Energy — James D. Watkins, 1989–
Secretary of Education — Lauro F. Cavazos, 1989–

VOTE

1988	Popular Vote	Electoral Vote
George H.W. Bush (Republican Party)	47,645,225	426
Michael Dukakis (Democratic Party)	40,797,905	111
Lloyd Bentsen (write in)	xx	1

ABOUT THE AUTHORS

CHARLES A. BEARD was born in Indiana and educated at De Pauw, Oxford, Cornell, and Columbia. He taught history and politics at Columbia for many years. He also wrote numerous important books and stirring articles dealing with history and government and became president of both the American Historical Association and the American Political Science Association.

Always concerned with quality in American politics and government, he became Director of the Training School for Public Service in New York City and conducted a number of important surveys of state and municipal governments. He also went abroad, upon request, to serve as a consultant on governmental affairs. His students included a number of men who later attained prominence in teaching and politics. He testified at Congressional hearings and was personally acquainted with presidents Wilson, Hoover, and Franklin D. Roosevelt.

Charles A. Beard's son, William, received his doctorate at Columbia University, taught political science, and entered the public service. He coauthored two books with his father; after the latter's death, he kept the Beard books current through timely revisions.

Charles A. Beard's daughter, Miriam Vagts, was a free-lance writer who wrote several books and many articles on historical subjects.

Her son, Detlev Vagts, is Bemis Professor of International Law at the Harvard Law School.

WITHDRAWN